EQUALS BEFORE GOD

*E*QUALS *before* *G*OD

Seminarians as Humanistic Professionals

*S*HERRYL *K*LEINMAN

THE UNIVERSITY OF CHICAGO PRESS

Chicago and London

Sherryl Kleinman is assistant professor of sociology at
the University of North Carolina.

The University of Chicago Press, Chicago 60637
The University of Chicago Press, Ltd., London
© 1984 by The University of Chicago
All rights reserved. Published 1984
Printed in the United States of America

93 92 91 90 89 88 87 86 85 84   54321

Library of Congress Cataloging in Publication Data

Kleinman, Sherryl.
  Equals before God.

  Bibliography: p.
  Includes index.
  1. Seminarians—United States—Psychology.
2. Professional socialization.   3. Humanism.   I. Title.
BV4030.K56   1984   305'.92   83-24208
ISBN 0-226-43999-2

TO MY PARENTS

CONTENTS

ACKNOWLEDGMENTS

Many people helped me bring this study to completion. I am indebted to Howard S. Becker for his support throughout the project. He coached me on matters of methodology and writing and provided valuable comments on drafts of the manuscript. Discussions with and comments from Gary Alan Fine were significant in shaping the work; I have benefited much from our colleagueship. In his inimitable style, the late Gregory P. Stone asked challenging questions and scrutinized early drafts of the manuscript. Michal M. McCall made excellent suggestions for rearranging material in a later draft.

The following people helped in many ways: Howard Aldrich, Judith M. Bennett, Patricia Bryan, Geraldine Dawson, Thomas R. Dewar, Harold Finestone, Mary J. Gallant, Bruce R. Geyer, Joseph R. Gusfield, Lyle A. Hallowell, Kristina B. Hanan, David R. Heise, Lorraine H. Hoyt, Ellen M. McLamb, Barbara Rauschenbach, Patricia R. Sanford, Carol Schmid, Robert L. Scott, Sarah Sherer, Susan Smith-Cunnien, Barbara Stenross, Judy Via.

Special thanks are due the people of Midwest Seminary; they generously shared their time and experiences with me.

I dedicate this book to my first teachers, Bella and Hy Kleinman.

ix

1

The Context of Deprofessionalization

> Professionals *profess*. They profess to know better than
> others the nature of certain matters, and to know better
> than their clients what ails them or their affairs. This is
> the essence of the professional idea and the professional
> claim.
>
> —Everett C. Hughes, "Professions"

Occupations holding the honorific title "profession" have convinced the public that their practitioners can deliver an esoteric service, determined and justified by knowledge systematically created and applied to their clients' problems. This knowledge—the professional ideology—is taught in professional schools and is the basis of the profession's claim to know better than others, including its clients. Because professionals presumably know better, they expect their clients to trust them; only a professional can know when a colleague makes a mistake. Its presumed knowledge and authority renders the professional body an esteemed and distinctive occupation in the eyes of the public (Hughes 1971, 374; Becker 1970; Roth 1974).

The ministry once held this honorific title without question. As Hughes points out (1971, 375), the earliest meaning of the adjective "professed" described one who had "taken the vows of a religious order." Ministers were experts on morality, judges of goodness and sin in the everyday lives of their clients. Ministers' esoteric knowledge comprised not only special texts, such as the Bible, but spiritual experiences with the Divine. Their knowledge was informed by the transcendent, and their exclusive access to the transcendent gave them the authority to make moral prescriptions for their clients.

1

Deprofessionalization is "a loss to professional occupations of their unique qualities, particularly their monopoly over knowledge, public belief in their service ethos, and expectations of work autonomy and authority over the client" (Haug 1973, 197). This process may be set in motion when various publics begin to question or challenge professional claims to expertise and altruism. During the 1960s, for example, students questioned their educators' pedagogic skills and goodwill; poverty groups claimed to know more about their communities' needs than social workers, and black parents revolted against a school system dominated by white teachers (Haug and Sussman 1969).

Although some of these revolts have subsided, some sociologists hypothesize that more of the public will come to question professional claims in the future. Increased knowledge, brought about especially by computer technology, not only makes esoteric knowledge available to nonprofessionals but also demystifies professionals' expertise. With increasing knowledge and specialization, paraprofessionals do much of the work formerly done by professionals, thereby making if difficult to warrant a distinction between the two groups. Moreover, an increased emphasis on personalizing relations in recent times has led clients to redefine professional detachment as unconcern and to doubt professionals' claim to altruism (Sennett 1978; Haug 1973; Toren 1975).

Deprofessionalization is a hypothesis for the future, but challenges to the autonomy and authority of the ministerial profession actually began in the 1800s (Douglas 1977). The industrialization and democratization of American culture established the situation in which "modern consciousness" arose. The spread of modern consciousness, which questioned the "God-givenness" of institutions, and moral relativism, which questions the moral absoluteness of world views, led to challenges to the validity and vitality of the ministry's services and knowledge. In premodern societies, institutions are characterized by "a very high degree of taken-for-granted certainty"; people experience traditional institutions "almost as objective as the facts of nature" (Berger 1979, 13). Consequently, people also experience their sense of self anchored in those institutions as fate, rather than as a matter of choice.

Modernity, on the other hand, has made the institutional network of society more complex than it was. This is true not only for the division of labor and technological advances, but more important for our purposes, for the choices individuals must make. Modernity pluralizes (ibid., 15). This means that people are no longer faced with only a few programs for human activity but with a wide range of programs. In such a society, people can no longer experience a particular institution as objectively given, as a matter of fate. Rather, by being confronted with a variety of institutions, people begin to sense that there is no single way to be or live, but a number of ways from which they may choose.

With a perception of social structures as relative, people begin to experience the immanent or immediate, rather than the transcendent, as the basis for reality. As Sennett notes: "As the gods fled, immediacy of sensation and perception grew more important; phenomena came to seem real in and of themselves as immediate experience" (1978, 151). In addition, by no longer using external structures as the basis for reality, people increasingly began to turn to themselves for deciding what is truth: "If answers are not provided objectively by [the] society, [people are] compelled to turn *inward*, toward their own subjectivity, to dredge up from there whatever certainties [they] can manage" (Berger 1979, 20).

Modern consciousness and moral relativism challenge the very existence of the Church as an institution and the traditional ministry as a profession. In premodern societies, people experience all institutions as God-given. Since religion, however, is an area where people expect to be provided with God-given truths, the emergence of a variety of religious world views probably created an even greater crisis of confidence in people's belief in objective reality than the pluralizing of other institutions. Each institution that legitimated itself as a religion—that claimed access to ultimate truth—was seen as providing only one version of it. The pluralizing of conventionally religious institutions put the whole notion of ultimate truth into question.

The sense of relativism that modernization creates and the notion that reality is based more on the immanent than the transcendent threatened conventional religious institutions. This threat was amplified in the late 1800s, when the disestablishment of the clergy (separation of church and state) occurred. The churches no longer had a guaranteed source of support.

Between 1820 and 1875, the Protestant Church in this country was gradually transformed from a traditional institution which claimed with certain real justification to be a guide and leader to the American nation to an influential *ad hoc* organization which obtained its power largely by taking cues from the non-ecclesiastical culture on which it was dependent. (Douglas 1977, 25)

RESPONSES TO THE CHALLENGE

The Protestant clergy, certain segments of it in particular, responded to the beginning of deprofessionalization by developing an ideology that accommodated the modern situation. They used relativistic ideas and the "secular" movement toward personalizing relations—the very forces that had led others to question the authority of ministers' knowledge and skills—to reestablish their work as a valued occupation.

The clergy gradually developed a humanistic professional ideology, role, core activity, and rhetoric of autonomy.[1] Their "new theology" relativized religion as one world view among many and suggested that there is no distinction between mundane and sacred realities, "for all of life is of ultimate significance" (Hiller 1969, 184). In addition, the subjective and personal became the basis for religious reality. The "new ministers" are counselors rather than preachers or moral standard setters. Their role is both personal and egalitarian—ministers treat their clients like peers. The new rhetoric of professional autonomy centers on "community"; their use of the term suggests that religion is open to anyone and that clients need not adhere to strict religious rules. To call the ministry a community is also to suggest that it is a distinctive and esteemed professional body.

1. "Humanism," an ideology that calls for personalized and egalitarian relations among people may be contrasted with "traditionalism." My usage of the humanistic and the traditional is similar to Sanders' and Lyon's (1976) distinction between traditional and nontraditional artists. They do not specify, however, the personal and egalitarian dimensions of the concept.

PROBLEMS ARISING FROM THE
CLERGY'S RESPONSE

Paradoxes

The ministry's new ideology contains a paradox, since to suggest that their knowledge is merely a world view and that clients as well as ministers are religious experts denies their own moral authority. Although the ideology suggests that religion has a place in modern society, its distinctiveness becomes questionable if the transcendent no longer exists. If religious professionals are counselors, then clients might well consult a psychological therapist instead. With the definition of the ministerial role as personal and egalitarian, clients may seek help from friends rather than their minister. If the autonomy of the profession is based on a vague notion of community, clients might well join some other community instead.

Parishioners

Humanism seems to be at odds with the public's, especially many parishioners', current expectations of ministers. The humanistic professional ideology was supposed to please modern parishioners. Ironically, those ideas seem to be ahead of parishioners, who hold more traditional expectations of ministers than ministers hold for themselves. For example, in their survey of 3,089 ministers and 1,806 lay people in Canada and the United States, Schuller, Brekke, and Strommen found that clergy share

the sense of need to create a setting for the active participation of people. . . . It is interesting that professional church leaders appeared more sensitive to this dimension of ministry than laity who might benefit from this type of ministry. Most laity, it seems, still perceive of the minister as the chief actor in the church, a professional who carries out certain functions. . . . Many of the congregation still view themselves primarily as spectators rather than as ones mutually called to share a ministry with others. (1975, 73)

Their study suggests that a social lag exists between the views of some segments of the clergy and those of some segments of the laity; each has changed in different ways and at a different pace. Consequently, some clergy and parishioners today have conflicting views of how ministers should think and act.

The general process of deprofessionalization led many parishioners to leave the Church, and the Church responded by humanizing its practitioners' role. But since the challenging of religious authority probably changed at different rates for different people, those who stayed with the Church (as an institution and tradition) were probably those least affected by the processes of modernity and, hence, most traditional. In addition, because of the pressures of modernity, those who cling to the traditional view today may exaggerate their traditional expectations of ministers. These parishioners may in fact compartmentalize religion in the modern era, setting religious activity aside for a few hours a week in church. Because religion is no longer a world view that informs their everyday activity, they may rely on their minister—one symbol of religion—to make up for that lack. Parishioners may wish to live vicariously through their minister's religiosity which, they assume, goes on all week in many situations. From their point of view, a guitar-playing, humanistic minister may not suffice as a collective representation of religion.

Significantly, people who teach in graduate professional schools of theology may have different notions of how to be religious than parishioners: "Typically, parish ministers reflected views much closer to the laity regarding which competencies are central to ministry than did seminary professors and students" (ibid., 83). Those who teach in seminaries are more likely to keep up with, and be responsive to, developments in theology than parishioners. Since the latest trend is the "new theology" (Hiller 1969), it is understandable that these ministers' ideas about "the religious" differ from those of people outside the academic community. As in other professional training schools, the faculty have different notions about what is important to learn than practitioners do, and both groups share different notions than clients (Becker et al., 1961; Freidson 1970b). In medical school, for instance, faculty are often research oriented, while students (and practitioners) share with clients a more clinical orientation.

Socialization

The ministry's response to deprofessionalization has produced dilemmas of socialization for its future practitioners. Seminarians in programs that present the humanistic ideology, role, and rhetoric are learning to be professionals by adopting an ideology that walks a thin line between providing an image of the ministry as an esteemed profession and undermining its own authority. Students cannot be certain that they are learning an esoteric service based on esoteric knowledge and question whether they will "know better" than their clients. They have trouble identifying with their occupational role, tasks, knowledge, and ideology.

Before describing a seminary and the socialization problems that this book analyzes, let us examine the new role, religion, and rhetoric more closely.

THE "NEW" THEOLOGY

Throughout this book I treat religion as a folk construct (Turner 1957), rather than as a scientific or sociological construct. Religion, then, is a set of beliefs, expectations, and meanings that people share within a community and consciously recognize as a religion. This definition is itself a product of modernization but allows us to study changes in people's meanings over time instead of judging which meaning systems deserve to be called "religious."[2] From this view, certain meaning systems that people do not initially define as religious may later become legitimated as religions; or, if the category becomes devalued more generally in a society, groups with particular ideologies may dissociate themselves from religion and call what they do something else instead (for example, "therapy").

In responding to the modern situation, theologians may "reaffirm the authority of the tradition in defiance of the challenges

2. Sociologists have tried to define religion in order to determine whether it has disappeared in modern times or is here "invisibly" (see Bellah 1964; Luckmann 1967; Wilson 1976; Bell 1979; Greeley 1972; Hiller 1969; Miller 1975). I have found that sociologists often use religion as both a scientific and an evaluative construct, usually positive. It is not the task of the social scientist to judge which meaning systems are "truly" religions. By treating religion as a folk construct, one can study changes in groups' definitions of the term and the consequences of those changes.

to it; . . . secularize the tradition; . . . uncover and retrieve the experiences embodied in the tradition" (Berger 1979, xi; see also
Gilkey 1967). I am not suggesting that Church officials and theologians cynically went about saving the institution. As Berger
points out, because theologians are the very people who take religious knowledge seriously, they felt the "cognitive pressure" to
deal with the former "objective" quality of religion in a situation
of pluralism (1979, 54).

In graduate professional schools of theology, it appears that secularizing the tradition (what Berger calls "reduction") has been
the most popular adaptation to change. Reduction is an attempt
to get rid of the stigma of having knowledge that others perceive
as invalid or no longer appropriate to the times. It involves trans-
lating the previous knowledge into terms that are acceptable. In
accord with the dominant trend toward personalizing relations
and "turning inward," psychologistic vocabularies have become
popular among the clergy. Reduction is part of what Hiller has
termed the New Theology:

While there is not a systematic body of knowledge that is recognized
among theologians as the new theology, . . . the primary characterization
of this development . . . is succinctly contained in the term "secularization," whereby liberation is obtained from rigid and closed religious
worldviews, and the world is accepted as a sanctioned ground for action.
(1969, 180)

From this perspective, all people are defined as part of God's
reality. As Shinn stated in his discussion of the theologian Karl
Barth:

God's affirmation of man in Christ is an affirmation of humanity—not of
good men or religious men or Christian men. Barth has no interest in the
various religions and irreligions of the world, but he is interested in *men*
of all religions and no religions. Christians are not more human and not
more loved of God than anyone else. (1968, 38)

We see in this new theology elements of the relativizing that
brought conventional notions of religion into question in the first
place. The new theology questions the existence of a transcendent
religious sphere separate from mundane reality, which formerly
provided the basis for the clergy's authority and expertise. By
obliterating the distinction between mundane and transcendent

reality, between believers and nonbelievers, religion is demysti-
fied, thereby accommodating the dominant reality.[3]

REDEFINING THE PROFESSIONAL
ROLE AND CORE ACTIVITY

In theory, the demystification of religion expands its content to
include everything and makes it available to everyone. Further, everyone becomes, by virtue of existing, a "religious expert." What,
then, is the professional role of the minister and the core activity
of the profession?

Ministers become counselors. While such a role may seem new
and particularly "unreligious" to some, the clergy helped people
solve interpersonal problems long before the rise of psychological
therapies:

During the first half of this century, and especially in the mid-century, the
personalist mode of intervention acquired an unprecedented and entirely
secular version . . . . This period saw the secularization of personal care,
or to put it with more caution, *the emancipation of professional and personal care from pastoral care.* (Halmos 1978, 49; my emphasis)

The establishment of pastoral counseling as the core activity of
the modern clergy made sense for four reasons. First, there is a
close relationship between counseling and Christian ethics (Halmos 1966). Second, although some have argued that the rise of
science has been responsible in part for the decline of institution-
alized religion, the association of pastoral counseling with such
fields as psychiatry has lent a scientific air to the ministry: "Coun-
selling thus adds the essential aura of scientism to pastoral care,
thereby making it more relevant and acceptable in the dominant,
secular, everyday world" (Leat 1973, 563). Third, because what
used to be called spiritual problems are now socially defined as
mental-health problems, pastoral counselors can keep them within
the pastoral province while giving them the popular definition. Finally, although the pastor's role is general, counseling provides the
ministers with a seemingly specialized skill.

3. A similar understanding of religion took hold in Catholicism after Vatican II
(see Hammersmith 1976; Ebaugh 1977; Goldner, Ference, and Ritti 1973).

How does the new professional role differ from the old? Traditionally, to become a professional was to acquire an honorific "real self" along with the honorific title.[4] Put a little differently, the person's experience of real self was anchored in, determined by, the institutional role or title. Others expected a professional to "act like a professional," even in situations unrelated to professional work; they treated the person as if the title indicated who the professional was "really." Those professionals who embraced their role may indeed have anchored their "real selves" in the institutional title.

Turner (1976) has argued that people have come increasingly to root their real selves and sense of what is real in impulse rather than in institutions. People tend to feel more "like themselves" in out-of-role behavior than in following institutionally grounded rules. They wish to exhibit role distance from both structural identities (e.g., worker, professional) and interpersonal identities (e.g., friend, lover, parent). Sennett (1978) specifies that people have come to feel most like themselves in interpersonal rather than structural relations. People, then, not only feel that the "impulsive" is more "real" than the institutional, but also associate the former with interpersonal relations. People consider the private realm as the arena where they can "be themselves," "let go," "let their hair down." Within the new framework, people define institutional roles as masks that hide the true face of the individual. There is a clear value judgment here—institutional roles are bad because they are fake, inauthentic; people search for the personality behind the mask.

If Sennett and Turner are correct, then people today will value structural relations (e.g., client-professional relationship) that are also interpersonally oriented—what we might call personalized structural relations. (For example, when people say their job is alienating and impersonal, their judgment suggests that they expected intimacy in the public realm.) In the process of losing their impersonal basis of authority, ministers increasingly came to use the newly valued personality as the basis for their new role and their structural relations with clients. The traditional understanding of the professional identity suggested that the structural role

4. "Role self" and "real self" are used here as folk constructs, not sociological concepts (see Katz 1972; Turner 1976, 1978).

of professional provided the individual with a valued "real self." In the humanistic understanding of the ministerial identity, expressiveness and the modern "real self" of interpersonal relations become the basis for the professional role. The new professional, like the old, acquires a real self. But, before, the role was seen as determining the person; now, the person determines the role.

Further, although people can use charisma to establish inequality in their interpersonal relations, modern notions of being oneself require acceptance, tolerance, and equality in interpersonal relations. As Stone (1970) puts it, people are concerned with "mood" in interpersonal relations; they tend to be expressive and appreciative of each other. In structural relations, people are concerned with "value"; they appraise each other. In personalizing their professional role, ministers have become appreciative rather than critical of others. Ministry students learn to establish rapport with clients, to "affirm" rather than judge them. Because self-disclosure becomes the new moral good (Sennett 1978), the new ministers are not supposed to define what their clients say as bad; the only morally bad action is to refrain from revealing personal information. Hence, the new structural role is nonjudgmental, appreciative, and supportive.

The new role, then, springs from the modern basis for determining what is real (immanent appearances instead of the transcendent) and the kinds of relations that have become valued (the interpersonal). The ministers responded to challenges to their authority in the following way: they took on the private as an area of expertise by personalizing their relationship with their clients. They professionalized the personal by personalizing the professional.

COMMUNITY RHETORIC

The central term in the humanistic rhetoric is "community."[5] How did the ministry use "community" to relegitimate itself as a profession? The old "religious" basis of the ministerial profession has been questioned. The term "community," however, which was

5. Rhetoric is a "symbolic means of inducing cooperation in beings that by nature respond to symbols" (Burke 1962, 567).

traditionally associated with the churchly religions, has not lost its positive connotation among various groups. It is still a positive label that signifies the existence of a distinctive, special category of persons (Sennett 1978). The clergy, in reestablishing itself, has used and partially redefined a traditional word that also has modern appeal and an implicit notion of "specialness." In addition, people often use the term community in an abstract and ambiguous way (Brembeck and Howell 1952). The clergy could make the most of the flexibility of the term—they took a traditional word and used it to justify "specialness" on the basis of demystification. How was this accomplished?

Community once strictly defined the select few who were, perhaps, not only called but chosen for a religious life. In the humanistic view, the notion of community is expanded to include all those (ministers and parishioners) who treat others in personal and egalitarian ways. By expanding (some people might interpret it as loosening) the criteria for membership, the redefinition opens the possibilities that group members will no longer be seen or see themselves as distinctive and special. After all, one can argue that a host of other groups and communities offer the same or similar beliefs. Whether or not a group holds beliefs that are different from others', members may still use the term "community" to convince others that their group is distinctive. To call something a community is to *confer* group identity. Members can feel special without recognizing that their sense of specialness derives, in part, from the simple fact that they distinguish themselves from those outside their group. Thus, by a contradictory argument, the clergy have come to use "community" to convince others of their professional reestablishment—they are special by virtue of their demystification of the professional ideology.

At the level of the socializing organization, the term legitimates the occupation as a profession and at the same time fits modern, humanistic notions. Because socializers have linked "community" with being a good professional, they can also use the rhetoric to get students to take on humanistic beliefs and to participate in the measures designed to "better" them. The rhetoric has become, then, part of the new set of beliefs (humanism) and a means of social control.

MIDWEST SEMINARY

What follows is a study of the dilemmas of socialization experienced by students in a contemporary Protestant graduate school of theology. Midwest Seminary has a three-year Master of Divinity program that prepares men and women for the ordained ministry.[6] Almost all of the students live in dormitories on the seminary's campus.

During six months of field research in the academic year 1977–78, I participated in and observed as many of the daily activities of the ministry students as they, their teachers, and time permitted. I lived in one of the two student dormitories, went to classes in the seminary, ate with the students in the school cafeteria, attended chapel services, caucus meetings, "theologizing" groups, and special functions, and joined the students during their leisure time. I recorded detailed field notes as soon as possible after each "event," and I conducted open-ended, in-depth interviews (almost all tape-recorded) with thirty students of all levels, eight faculty, and two administrators. In addition to these interviews, my data consist of talks with many more respondents. These I recorded from memory. To guide my observations and interviews, I used the technique of theoretical sampling outlined in Glaser and Strauss 1967, deciding what to observe or who to talk to next on the basis of research questions and hypotheses that evolved in the field. I also examined documents such as newsletters, class handouts, a book on the history of the seminary, and ministry projects (discussed later).

Much of the literature on seminaries suggests that the change from traditional to more humanistically-oriented education is quite widespread, especially in graduate professional schools of theology (Carroll 1971). Wuthnow (1971) noted the trend toward "revisionist" ministries, and Fukayama (1972) refers to the "individualistic" style of ministry (see also Schuller, Brekke, and Strommen 1975). These authors distinguish new trends both from the more traditional and from the activist styles of ministry. The latter include clergy who sought to radically transform or

6. All names of persons and places are pseudonyms.

eradicate the Church as an institution during the late 1960s (see Garrett 1973; Nelsen, Yokely, and Madron 1973; Quinley 1974). At present, the humanistic, not the radical or the traditional style, characterizes most professional schools of the ministry.

It is not my intent, however, to generalize the findings from this study to other seminaries or professional schools. The deprofessionalization of the ministry is an extreme case, and it is possible that Midwest Seminary is more "liberal" than at least some other theological schools. This book is the first study of the consequences of deprofessionalization for the socialization of new professionals, and its contribution is in the atypicality of the situation studied. The atypical or unusual are important in studying social life because they highlight the general patterns we otherwise take for granted. By studying an extreme case, we will not only understand the problems that may arise in schools responding to deprofessionalization but also learn how *typical* professional programs assist their students in avoiding similar dilemmas. This "deviant case," then, can help us understand the process and potential problems of professional socialization.

2

Midwest Seminary

Midwest Seminary is a graduate professional school of theology affiliated with a major Protestant denomination and located on the campus of a large university in the midwestern United States, just a few miles from a city. While the seminary is not part of the university, the two organizations are associated. For the past fifty years, the seminary and the graduate school of the university have conducted a cooperative program in the advanced study of religion. Seminary students can use the health and recreational facilities of the university. However, most of the ministerial students have little contact with the university during their stay. For example, few students took courses at the university, used its library facilities, or ate in its cafeteria. Although faculty and students rarely made comments against the university or its students, students quickly learned that their place was Midwest Seminary, not the university. They learned, for example, to refer to Midwest Seminary as "the Community" (as if excluding other communities), and they used the word "campus" to refer to the seminary buildings and people, not the university.

The main building of the seminary contains classrooms, a chapel, a library, and some offices of the administrators, faculty, and staff. There is also another building that houses faculty offices.

The two residence halls for single students are located near the main building and housed most of the 195 ministry students, in single and double accommodations. I lived in the larger residence hall, which also contained the main lounge, bookstore, and cafeteria. Married students lived in one- and two-bedroom apartments a few blocks away. While the seminary did not approximate Goffman's 1961 portrayal of a total institution (his discussion relies heavily on coercive organizations), the students did sleep, play, and work in the same place. Further, this living arrangement affected how the organization could handle its legitimation problems. For example, it would have been more difficult for faculty and administrators to maintain that Midwest Seminary was a community and to suggest that students' competence as ministers would be chiefly determined by their day-to-day experiences in the seminary (rather than by "book learning") if the seminary had been a commuter school.

Generally, the atmosphere in the main building and in the residences was informal and friendly. Those who expect seminaries to resemble a monastery (as I did) would be surprised at their initial observations. Sociability is common during mealtimes in the cafeteria, especially at lunch, when faculty, students, and staff leave few seats unfilled. Because the cafeteria has only long tables, people who wish to eat together in private groups of two or three are usually unable to do so (at least at lunchtime). Although tables are somewhat "stratified" according to friendship group, race, and sex, students are likely to have to share a space with at least a few people outside their "group." Because of its sociable atmosphere, the cafeteria is one of the main places in which members of the new cohort meet each other and upper-level students. As one third-year female student said:

I find that a lot of socializing goes on over food. You first meet people sitting downstairs in the cafeteria and eating with people. And there you talk about anything; about what's going on in school, complain about the food, talk about how much work you've got. Over the table, over the food, you find out where people are from, what people are interested in and the normal preliminary chatter. You don't just go up to someone's door and say "Hi. I'm so and so." That doesn't happen at first, it evolves. (Interview)

The kind of relationship that this student alludes to does evolve among students and is most evident in interaction in dorm rooms and on dorm floors. The dorm I lived in housed students on three floors. Male students' rooms were on the first and third floors, and female students' rooms were on the second. Students visited each other often (both among and within floors), and male and female voices could be heard on all floors. This dorm accommodated most of the first-year students. About half of them shared a room with one other student, and the rest lived alone. The rooms were rather bare and dingy. Almost all the rooms (including those with one person) were small and furnished with two beds, two desks, two chairs, two lamps, and two closets. The walls of the rooms were painted either pale yellow, green, or beige, and the floors were tiled. Most of the students fixed up their rooms with colorful rugs, pillows, posters, bedspreads, and plants. Some students owned stereos, televisions, or radios. Although fire regulations prohibited the use of certain electrical appliances, most students had hot pots to make coffee, tea, cocoa, or soups, and a few had more elaborate cooking appliances. Some students rented small refrigerators. The uneven distribution of these resources provided students with opportunities to share them. They borrowed each other's utensils and used them for collective events. For example, since the cafeteria was closed on weekends, students often pooled resources (food, money, utensils) to make their meals in their rooms. On my floor, the woman who lived in the next room (and who owned the most elaborate cooking appliances in the seminary) often invited me and five or six other students to her room for a potluck dinner on Sunday evenings. Other groups of two to seven students did the same. Students sometimes ate in restaurants in the surrounding area but could not afford to do so often. Further, people would gather in each other's rooms to watch a favorite television show. "Helping out" was a common activity, and it did not only occur among close friends. Students often helped each other with classwork, offered car rides, and borrowed various items. I, too, participated in this give and take.

The Program

Midwest Seminary offers various degrees, including the Master of Divinity (a three-year program for those pursuing the ordained ministry), the Master of Christian Education (for those pursuing the educational ministry of the Church, such as sunday school teachers), the Master of Theological Studies (for persons who wish to study theology but not enter the professional ministry), the Doctor of Ministry, and in conjunction with the university, the M.A. and Ph.D. degrees in religion (conferred by the university). Approximately sixty-five percent of the three hundred students are enrolled in the ministry program, twenty percent are doctoral students, and the remainder are special or nondegree students. The seminary offers "professional" (M.Div.) and "advanced" (Ph.D.) degrees, but the recruits who are pursuing the ordained ministry are treated, and see themselves, as separate from the Ph.D. students. Though not all ministerial students live on the seminary campus, no doctoral students do. Also, doctoral students take different courses at the seminary and must accumulate a certain number of credits at the university. I did observe and interview some Ph.D. students, but I was interested in them only as they became relevant to the students in the three-year Master of Divinity program.

Admission requirements for the M.Div. include a degree from an accredited college or university, "acceptable academic performance" (quoted in school catalog, 1977–78), and letters of recommendation from the student's school or church. The catalog does not specify a minimum grade point average, and students generally feel that the school accepts most people who apply to the program. Further, as mentioned in the catalog, the school accepts students with wide-ranging backgrounds, including the liberal arts, natural sciences, and social sciences. The admissions committee considers applicants' volunteered or paid work experience in the Church or other "service" organizations, as well as their "personal statement of goals," an important part of the application.

The three-year program (nine terms of ten-week periods) includes a number of "area requirements." Of the thirty-one courses required for the degree, students must take two courses in biblical studies, two in historical studies, two in theology, one in ethics and society, one in pastoral psychology and pastoral care, and one in preaching. Students must also have two field education experiences, with at least one in a local parish setting. During field education, the student (alone or on a team with peers) works about twenty hours a week at a nearby church, institution, or community agency. In the parish setting, the student acts as assistant or associate pastor. Because students usually "do field ed." on the weekends, they sometimes refer to themselves as "weekend warriors." They participate in two-hour, small-group advisory sessions at the seminary each week, led by a member of the field education department. Most students opt for "Clinical Pastoral Education" as one of their two experiences. For this requirement, students work as chaplains (under supervision) often in a hospital or prison. Before attempting CPE, they take a series of psychological tests and interviews at the assessment service of the seminary. Students often undergo psychological testing in one form or another during their three years. For example, they take psychological and vocational tests a week before classes begin (in the first year of study) and also before interning. About ten percent of the students take the intern-year option, usually after the second year of study. The intern participates full time in ministry (under professional supervision) at a parish, institution, or agency for nine to twelve months.

During the first year, students take a required course called "Introduction to Ministry." Here, each professor meets with new advisees (about eight) every week. It is unclear what is supposed to go on during these sessions (as they are sometimes called), but faculty and students sometimes described them as "support groups" or "primary identification groups."

Also during the first year, students write a ministry project, a twenty-page paper in which they express their "personal goals and understandings of the ministry" (quoted from the one-page document which describes it). Faculty and administrators define this hurdle as the most important requirement of the first year, a test which presumably not only measures students' technical competence but also their fitness for the role of minister. Consequently, students take this task very seriously and worry about it until it is completed and evaluated by two members of the faculty in spring term.

There are two other assessments of competency, one in each remaining year. At the end of the second year, students attend the evaluation conference, conducted by the student's adviser, the field supervisor, and one other faculty member. For this meeting, the student submits a transcript, the first-year ministry project, the field supervisor report, some papers and projects, a revised statement of the ministry project, an annotated bibliography of books and articles of the student's choosing, and a statement outlining the student's plans for the third year of study. To an outsider, this second assessment seems more formidable than the first. However, faculty and administrators put so little emphasis on it (compared to the first-year project), that students attend to it with little fuss and anxiety. Finally, the students meet their advisers during the next to last term for a final evaluation. The student writes a "statement of faith" for this senior consultation as well as a report which includes a statement of plans for continuing self-education following graduation.

Since the early 1970s, the seminary has expressed an official commitment to three "special concerns" (in school catalog, 1977–78): (1) the Church and the black experience, (2) the role of women in Christian ministry, and (3) peace and world community. There are courses offered in these areas, and the seminary has a black student caucus and a women's student caucus. Some of these changes were instituted to deal with the political radicalism of Midwest Seminary students during the 1960s. At that time, students demonstrated to change the curriculum. However, it was also during the 1960s that people began to seek psychological solutions to political problems (see Halmos 1966), and the seminary was no exception. Hence, while students discuss feminism, racism, world peace, or the Church and homosexuality, they tend to translate these public issues into psychological problems or "feeling states." Midwest Seminary might not be more liberal than other graduate schools of theology. However, because of the presumed "social problems" emphasis of the three special concerns and the presence of returning doctoral students who talk about the "radical" activities they participated in as M.Div. students in the 1960s, most of the ministerial students think they are at a very progressive seminary.

Midwest Seminary confers the M.Div., but the Church ordains the students. Consequently, while the students pursue the degree, they must also satisfy the Church's requirements for ordination. Each student is linked with the Church at the levels of the local church, the district, and the state, or conference. A committee of pastors at each level examines and interviews their prospective candidates. Of the three, students have the most contact with the district committee. This committee assigns a supervising pastor to each student, who meets with him or her about once a month and sends a report on the candidate's progress to the district committee. Students meet with their district committee about three times a year, at which time members may question them about theology or personal matters. In order to determine if the student is fit for ordination, the annual conference board of ordination of the state reads the application for ordination, as well as the supervising pastor's report, and meets with the student. Conferences differ in their requirements.

Most students are ordained deacons well before they graduate, usually during their second year of study. This title allows them to assume certain ministerial duties—they may baptize or marry people and administer the sacraments. The Church, then, confers the title on the students before the school certifies them. As far as I could tell, the faculty do not treat ordained students differently from those who have not yet reached that stage. In many cases, faculty are unaware that a student has received deacon's orders. The school, then, does not guide students through the steps to ordination, but expects them somehow to know how to do it. In a few cases, students did not find out what they should do until quite late and had to meet all the Church committees in a short period of time in order to be ordained by a certain date. Therefore, while the seminary receives legitimacy, services, and funds from the Church, the ministerial student must deal with the two systems as separate bodies. Further, my data indicate that despite all the Church's requirements for ordination and the fact that it, not the school, confers the title of minister, students remain more sensitive to what their teachers and peers think and do. Since the students receive their training in the school rather than in the Church, this is not surprising.

The People

The people of Midwest Seminary include the students, faculty, administrators, and staff. I will briefly describe these groups; their interrelationships will become clear in my analysis in later chapters.

Most of the students are in their middle- to late- twenties, although there are also some second-career, or "mature," students. About thirty percent of the students during the 1977–78 academic year were women, most of whom were studying for the Master of Divinity degree. About twelve percent of the students were black. Most of the students came from middle- to lower-middle-class backgrounds and grew up in small towns or cities in the Midwest. Many of them received undergraduate degrees from denominational colleges or universities, although they were quick to point out in interviews that little was "religious" about the colleges they attended. Many had participated in various church activities, though some had had minimal contact with "organized religion" since preadolescence. Most were affiliated with a particular denomination, but students also came from more than a dozen other Protestant denominations. Undergraduate backgrounds were varied and included music, medicine, education, sociology, and philosophy. Students were surprised to discover that only a small percentage of their peers had majored in religion or philosophy as undergraduates.

There are approximately thirty full-time faculty members, of whom three are (white) females and four are black (males). All have received either the Ph.D., the D.Div., or Th.D. degrees, many from prestigious universities. Almost all are ordained.

The administration includes the president, dean, assistant to the president, director of development, business manager, and the director of student affairs. One of the newest members of the administration has recently (since 1977) made some changes in the program and has put a special emphasis on the development of interpersonal skills and the "personhood" of students. "Interpersonalism" was emphasized in the seminary before that time, but this administrator has tried to institutionalize it. For example, although the "Introduction to Ministry" course existed before 1978 in a different form, he made sure that the "support groups" remained small and called them by that name. Also, despite the fact that psychological testing was already part of the program, he introduced testing into the program even before the start of classes for the new cohort.

There are eight members of the administrative council and about forty members of the office and maintenance staff, most of whom the students and faculty recognize by name and face. It should be noted that many students are also staff members in that they work part time in the cafeteria, library, bookstore, buildings and grounds, and reception area. These are sources of income for the students, some of whom also receive funds from their home church or conference.

3

The Humanistic Role

Traditionally, ministers were supposed to be personable, but not personal, with their clients and assumed an authoritative demeanor. The nonegalitarian and impersonal aspects of the role are linked in that professionals' authority is partly sustained by their impersonal manner. By keeping their relationships with nonprofessionals (inside and outside the work setting) on an impersonal level, professionals also refrain from showing they are like ordinary people with human flaws.

The humanistic role calls for personal and egalitarian relations between professionals and their clients. Students learn that their personal qualities largely determine whether they will be good ministers and that they should become involved with clients rather than remain emotionally distant. However, it is possible to per-

Sections of chapter 3 were published in Sherryl Kleinman and Gary Alan Fine, "Rhetorics and Action in Moral Organizations: Social Control of Little Leaguers and Ministry Students," *Urban Life* 8, no. 3 (October 1979):275–94, copyright © 1979; and in Sherryl Kleinman, "Making Professionals into 'Persons': Discrepancies in Traditional and Humanistic Expectations of Professional Identity," *Sociology of Work and Occupations* 8, no. 1 (February 1981):61–87, copyright © 1981. Both articles are reprinted by permission of Sage Publications, Inc.

sonalize the professional-client relationship without making it egalitarian. For example, some service professionals liken their relationship with clients to that between a parent and child (Halmos 1970). These counselors are affectively involved with their clients but still see themselves as better, more mature people. In short, people may use their personal style to establish authority with others (Swidler 1979).

The new ministers are trying to fashion a personal role that is supposed to produce a relationship of equality between themselves and their clients. By redefining their role to include this egalitarian dimension, they demystify the traditional conception of the professional as superior or extraordinary. According to their beliefs, the minister is a human being with human frailties as well as talents.

The new core activity is counseling, referred to as "ministering." Ministering, however, becomes more than counseling skills; it is a matter of being a helpful, caring person. Students learn that they not only minister to clients, but their clients also minister to them. This is the sense in which professional-client encounters are egalitarian; the minister is expected to reveal personal information during encounters with clients and to receive as well as give help. The students learn that all people have talents and can be good people; hence, clients, too, are capable of ministering to others, including the minister.

How do faculty teach students to take on the humanistic role?

LEARNING TO BE HUMANISTS

Much like those in traditionally oriented professional programs, students learn to merge the professional "role self" and their "real self." For example, in a female student's room one evening, with five women present, one woman said:

Being a minister is your life. It's not like other professions. There's no difference between the pastor and person. They're the same. [The four other women nodded.] (Field notes)

But unlike traditional professionals, students learn that their personal identity creates the role, not vice versa. In this organization, students acquire the notion that they must use their "total personality" in ministering and that personal qualities determine how good a minister they will be. Faculty and administrators make interpersonal relations a value by telling recruits that education is not limited to the classroom and that day-to-day interactions with students, faculty, and staff are just as important, if not more important, than the formal curriculum. During orientation week, an administrator said to the incoming class:

We like to think holistically here. Courses are only benchmarks. . . . Your real work comes when you talk to individual professors and students. Get to know the professors, their gifts. . . . If it's person-centered, you will really learn. (Field notes, Fall 1978)

Seminary faculty and administrators tell the students that their role is not given, but shaped, and they, not the school, are primarily responsible for creating it. It is the organization, however, that directs the shaping of the new role, and the rhetoric of "personal responsibility" for role making in fact means that faculty and administration expect students to cooperate with the organizational measures designed to "better" them. The organization works on bettering the students in a variety of ways. During orientation week, new students are given a series of personality and vocational tests, the results of which are discussed with the assessor, the student, and the student's adviser. In the first year of study, all students participate in small group discussions "facilitated" by a member of the faculty. Faculty define these as support groups, and social and theological issues are discussed mainly in personal terms. In the first year of study, and in some upper-year courses, faculty ask students to keep a journal in which they write "personal reflections" on theological and other matters. Each student submits a ministry project at the end of the second term of study. The ministry student's "person" is worked on further through a series of psychological tests and personal interviews that must be taken before internship as a chaplain.

Socializers say that what recruits learn is central to their "personhood" and that only the person who is "whole" can make a

good minister. This is part of the official rhetoric. The school catalog, for example, specifies that the program not only provides its
students with intellectual and practitioner skills but helps them
achieve a higher level of "personhood" as well. An administrator
described the ministry project as the most important requirement
of the first year of study:

The ministry project is an honesty statement. This is where you grasp
yourself, see what you're doing, grasp yourself in ministry. . . . Getting
your ministry project together is the most important thing in your first
year, more important than grades. A student who doesn't come to grips
with his ministry but has all As has failed, in my opinion. (Field notes:
orientation speech, Fall 1978)

One professor described the project this way:

[Students] have to show—and that's the whole point—that they can integrate [academic material] with their commitments, their own sense of
identity, who they are. (Interview)

Congruent with modern notions, students learn that there is a
split between most institutional "role selves" and people's "real
selves," and that the role self is artificial compared with the real
self. Professors teach students that the traditional role is artificial,
although real in its consequences. For example, in answer to a student's question, "How is pastoral psychotherapy different from
regular psychotherapy?" the professor said:

Pastoral psychotherapy is therapy done by a pastor. I know that sounds
simplistic, but that's what it is. It depends on whether you are recognized
as a pastor by others. Where I come from, they used to talk about the
office of the minister, what they now call role, I guess. The role invites a
certain interaction, it interferes with the interaction. . . . If you depend
on the mantle for your personality, then it becomes a corset. You need
your own personality. (Class field notes)

Socializers talk about the ideal minister in terms of self or person, not role. For example, in a class on the founder of the denomination of the school, the professor argued that students
should study him as a person instead of only analyzing his works.
To emphasize a person's work is presumably to value role performance above the person:

People need to go through the kind of change [the founder] went through [from a rigid to a more flexible character], although less traumatic and dramatic. That's why I want you to keep a journal, because the journey for honesty and trust and self-awareness is crucial. (Class field notes)

Similarly, in preaching class, the professor encouraged students to be human in the pulpit:

It's good for the congregation to see that even people into religion have problems. As my colleague [in the seminary] says, "Say as much as you can without unzipping yourself in front of the audience." (Class field notes)

Professors, then, use the word "self" to refer to the good, humanistic, messages and reserve the term "role" to refer to the bad, traditional, messages. In conversations in the seminary and in interviews, students typically used role (or the titles minister, pastor, or Reverend) to describe outsiders' traditional stereotypes of ministers. They used self, person, or personal name to announce who they think they are. Every person I interviewed made this distinction during the interview or in other situations in the seminary. For example, a third-year student distinguished between being a professional and being a person:

I'm excited about ministering, but not about being a minister. [What's the difference?] The biggest difference is people's view of you. As a quote-unquote "professional pastor," I have a big stumbling block to get over, where I will never be accepted as common folk, but as Reverend Smith, which I hate. I am not Reverend Smith, I'm Bill, the person out there to minister to people, and who needs ministering to. . . . I'm still the same person. (Interview)

Note that this student distances himself from the traditional role of the minister by calling himself a "quote-unquote" 'professional pastor'." Another third-year student contrasted the title Reverend with her personal name:

I'm Joan regardless of whether they [parishioners] tack the Reverend on it or not. . . . On my intern year I dated one of the members of the church three different times and he never, *never* got beyond the point of calling me Reverend. Even on our dates! I kept saying, "Why don't you just call me Joan?" (Interview)

Students not only learn to contrast the traditional conception

of the minister with the "real self," but to use their personal identity as a basis for becoming a good minister. As one student wrote
in her ministry project:

I came to [Midwest Seminary] thinking that here I would be "trained to
be a minister." But I've discovered there is much more to the making of a
minister than learning particular skills. First and foremost this year I have
discovered that I am finding myself—what it means to be Dorothy Mac-
Rae: woman, Christian, minister.

In twenty-one of twenty-three ministry projects I examined, the
students wrote about their conception of being a minister as a
"real self" anchored in interpersonal relations. Students also talked
about being a minister this way in interviews, informal talks, and
in seminars.

My dorm door was ajar and I heard some talk going on in the hallway. I
peeked out and saw three second-year students talking. Mary was in the
middle of saying, in a somewhat exasperated but endearing tone, "This
place'll drive you crazy!" I said, "Hmm, really?" Mary laughed and said,
"Yah!" Jim said, "Sure. In other graduate schools you can just regurgitate
back. In scripture class, for instance, you could just learn the passages.
But, you'll be asked how that passage affected your life. You can't just
learn information, you have to relate it to *you*." Mary said, "Yes, it's a total
involvement. It's a community. You eat here and sleep here and go to
classes here. You're always in touch with everyone." (Field notes)

Faculty pass on the egalitarian aspect of the role by communicating the idea that ministers are like other people—they are human. These ministry students learn that they have human frailties
(as well as gifts) and that they must try to better themselves in
order to minister to those in need.

Students are supposed to better themselves, but they are not
supposed to act like moral elitists, as traditional expectations dic-
tate. From the humanistic viewpoint, the ideal person is one who
recognizes the basic equality of all and cultivates personal attri-
butes that encourage relationships of equality. The expectations
may be summarized this way: ministry students should better
themselves while recognizing that they are really no better than
anyone else.

The traditional role perpetuates the mystification of the professional identity. By prescribing the personal-egalitarian role, Mid-

west's faculty call into question the professionalism of the ministerial identity. Revealing personal information is out-of-role behavior for professionals and can decrease the social distance between the professional and the client (Kadushin 1962). The professors, almost all of whom are ordained, portray the minister as human (and, therefore, equal) by revealing details about themselves that would likely be absent from classrooms in more traditional settings. For example:

Professor Robinson talked about himself as a father, husband, teacher, and friend in class, saying that he couldn't exist as a person without these identities. He talked about how he has changed over the years, saying that he is at peace with himself now. He talked about how his life style has changed. I noted that his talk about himself in relation to others reminded me of the way the ministry students talk. (Field notes)

Other times, professors make explicit links between revealing the self, creating the personal-egalitarian role, and demystifying the traditional identity. For example, in another class the professor said:

The pastor is lonely and needn't be. But part of the loneliness is that working with the congregation means they'll find out you're not doing anything special or holy. But it's worth the sharing. (Field notes)

The humanistic role directs the professional to participate with, rather than lead, clients. Some faculty encourage students to develop participatory worship services and innovative types of ministry.

To merge the role self and real self is also to establish the ministerial identity as transsituational. Similar to conventional notions about the professional role as one which makes the incumbent special in all situations, the new ministerial role makes all encounters relevant to the identity. Faculty teach recruits that learning (in this case, personalizing) occurs everywhere and that what they learn, the values, norms, and behaviors they acquire, are generalizable to all situations. Recruits see their time in the seminary as providing them the opportunity to develop a way of life, and this way of life is the context within which technical, situationally based tasks of learning are placed. Hence, recruits learn that they are not merely acquiring a role self—a mask that can be put on or taken off depending on the situation—but discovering a real self.

Socialization Problems

The humanistic role poses problems for students for two main reasons. The first set of problems pertains to the role itself.

Role Problems

Personhood, the central idea in the role, is both vague and difficult to live out, for it involves revealing personal feelings and information in a variety of nonintimate contexts. With personhood and self-disclosure central, students do not have a professional role to hide behind. Although traditional professional programs may seem rigid, students there can shield their personal feelings and failings behind the impersonal authority of the professional role.

Students learn that being a good minister is being a good person. This puts tremendous pressure on them because every activity they engage in becomes relevant to the role and faculty and students constantly monitor each other's "goodness." There is no escaping the role. For example, a student too tired to attend a party may be considered a bad person and hence a bad minister-to-be:

Last night I asked Terry if she was going to the party. It was 10 P.M. and she was already in her nightgown. She said, "Oh, I partied all day." Terry is cutting herself off from people. She has a few close friends and that's it. Do you know about her appointment system? [No.] Well, if Terry wants to talk to you she sets up appointments, like "See you on Wednesdays at 1 to 1:30," that sort of thing. I don't think that's very pastoral. If someone wants to talk to you, you talk to them *then*, you don't set up appointments. (Field notes: female, first-year student)

In addition, by making self-disclosure important students sometimes feel hurt by what others say to or about them and experience a lack of privacy. Some students speak of seminary life as a fishbowl existence or say that they feel everyone wants to know their business.

Role in Context

The students' biggest problem results from the larger context in which they learn the humanistic role. Parishioners, parents, friends outside the seminary, and some Church board members have traditional expectations of ministerial students. Students at first are also outsiders, for they enter the program with traditional notions about what they will become. They acquire a traditional conception of the role of the minister long before they decide to go to seminary (Blizzard 1958). Through primary socialization, relationships in the community of their home church, and their associations with ministers, seminary students piece together conventional notions about how ministers are supposed to act.

They encounter people who mobilize traditional (impersonal, nonegalitarian) expectations of them. Once students announce their identity as minister or ministry student, others often (1) make the identity relevant to the interaction, (2) treat the individual as if "minister" were his or her primary identity, and (3) set the student apart as a moral superior or deviant. For example, consider the statement a second-year, female student made in an interview:

Ministers are watched. They are looked on as models and as examples. And whether it's fair or not, they are more or less expected by a lot of parishioners to be superhuman, perfect wonderpeople.

That people regard the student as a model indicates that, above all, she represents a "minister" to them. Further, the identity is, in Matza's (1969) term, "essentializing": people use it to conclude that the individual is (or should be) a "perfect person." All the students I interviewed talked about this. Lay people's expectations for ministers perhaps include more "don'ts" than "dos." Ministers are not supposed to engage in activities considered routinely deviant for others, such as having sex with certain others, dancing, smoking, drinking, or swearing. It is no surprise, then, that new students expect and fear that they will have to change their life style. Twenty-eight of the thirty students I interviewed were anxious about this. One second-year respondent even reported that he dreamt about his fear:

In the dream I'd be walking up to the door [of the seminary], put my hand on the doorknob, and then—nothing. I'd wake up. I was afraid to open that door. For me it symbolized the total "I don't know *what* I'm getting into up there." . . . I wondered, "What are they expecting of me, what kind of life style?" I felt threatened that I'd have to change my own personal life style. The fact that I drink occasionally, that I have a good time, I enjoy running around, I don't like to be tied down, I like my freedom.

A third-year student, a woman, said:

I wondered what it was going to be like up here with all these other people who were going to be ministers; wondering if there would be a lot of Fundamental-type people, if I could find people that I could have fun with, not thinking that if I'm going there, there should be other people similar.

Whether or not people think ministers are truly saints, they expect ministers to act as if they are morally superior. For example, in the community of their home church, the students receive what they believe to be undeserved respect from others. As one third-year woman put it:

And some of the older members of the church—they treated me with a lot more respect than what they might have otherwise [if I hadn't decided to become a minister]. I think people generally have an image of ministers. (Interview)

Friends are often less enthusiastic about their peer's choice of occupation but, like the parishioners of their home church, expect some change of behavior, that the student will no longer act like an equal, like "one of them."

Friends came out with the statement, "Oh, we never expected *you* to become a minister . . ." But once I came out with a point of view that was sort of radical, they thought it was OK. [What do you mean?] Oh, something contrary to what a minister is supposed to think. Whatever the issue, whether it be on homosexuality, abortion, or morality. Something left of center of the road. [They didn't already know how you stood on those issues?] Oh yeah, but that's reevaluated once they see you in quote-unquote "the light of a minister." (Interview: male, second-year student)

* * *

My friends did act strangely when they heard I was going to seminary. I remember that I stopped being asked to parties. When I talked with a few of my friends, they said they had stopped asking me because "you're a minister." They thought I might stop being *me* or something. (Interview: female, third-year student)

It appears that these friends feel that aspiring ministry students are the kind of people who are "above" partying, or think they are, and who will necessarily become less "liberal." The quotations also indicate that people force these students into the identity of minister even before they enter the seminary (Strauss 1969, 76).

Other evidence for outsiders' traditional notions of the ministerial role is shown by the fact that students who were considered "straight" by their friends and families did not receive reactions of surprise from outsiders at their decision to go to seminary:

I guess in some ways it wasn't surprising to people. Even when I worked in the hospital no one would tell dirty jokes around me. So people didn't treat me as different when I told them I was in seminary. I mean, even here, Billie [roommate], when she swears, says "I'm sorry, Val." Interview: female, second-year student)

*   *   *

The people I went to high school with weren't as surprised as the ones I went to college with. My high school friends all saw me as Reverend Hall. I was that way then. [What do you mean?] I was the one who was always starting prayer groups, having a Christian gospel singing group, and never did anything wrong. (Interview: male, second-year student)

Students, then, receive both positive and negative reactions from people outside the seminary. One second-year student I interviewed made the following statement about encountering others:

What I usually do is try and psyche out the person before I say I'm in seminary. I try and figure out if the person is someone who is going to get turned off by finding out, or if the person is going to put me on a pedestal.

This woman also alludes to students' problems of predicting others' responses. Ministry students discover that not only do friends, parents, teachers from college, and parishioners have different reactions, but there is variation within these groups. Some friends and former teachers are surprisingly supportive about the pursuit, while others are disappointingly negative. Parents do not always agree about their offspring's plans. A range of responses is common (Gustavus 1973):

I got mixed reactions. First, there were the people I told you about on campus [of a liberal arts college]. They said, "What do you want to do that for? You sure don't fit the stereotype of the minister." But other people thought it was great. I had just been sick with a serious illness and got better, so they thought God saved me or something, and that it was beautiful that I was going to be a minister. [Who were these people?] People at my home church. (Interview: male, first-year student)

Both positive and negative reactions indicate that (1) lay people expect ministers to appear like superordinates, either because they are "truly" morally enlightened or merely moralistic, and (2) people treat those who are pursuing the ministry as a career as if they have become converted to a new self that sets them apart from others.

People expect ministers and other professionals to be personable, but also to maintain an appropriate social distance from them. Consequently,

interaction . . . seldom goes beyond the minimal formal role requirements. While the minister may desire to move beyond this level of interaction and find out who his layman is as a person, and reveal to the layman that he is also a person, the layman is reluctant to do so because of the uncertainties of what this kind of relationship might lead to. (Hadden 1969, 215)

Ministry students learn that others expect them to depersonalize their relationships, containing emotions and restraining actions that would be considered appropriate in personal relations (or personalized structural relations). As one first-year student said in explaining his reluctance to become a minister:

Maybe I wasn't prepared to live a public life. . . . You have to be such a good example. People don't allow you to be yourself. You can't make mistakes. You can't have a flared temper.

The heterogeneity of responses within audiences intensifies the existing discrepancies as well as increases students' uncertainty about what it really means to be a minister. While many professors advocate or perform the humanistic role, some do not. Professors differ in their views of whether the seminary is primarily an academic graduate school of theology or a training school for ministers. The humanist/traditional split among the faculty generally falls along this applied/academic division. Not all professors are concerned about the presence or absence of a sense of community in the seminary, and some talk cynically about it:

[Some students talk about the seminary as a community.] That's the going phrase. [He sounded sarcastic.] Don't you start hearing talk about that in high school and you get into the school spirit? There, it's centered around athletic events and getting behind the team. It carries over into college. . . . Students want to come and find the school spirit in the seminary. [Do you think this is something the seminary should provide?] I think that students who get into seminary ought to be mature enough to provide their own community without whomping it up artificially. (Interview: faculty)

As one student put it, "Some faculty would cut up your paper if you handed in 'touchy-feely' theology."

Nor do examining and interviewing committees at the church, district, and state levels treat their future ministers uniformly. Some committees examine the students on theology, while others focus on interpersonal matters. Some expect candidates to justify their claims to the identity in terms of a traditional calling:

The district committee feels that if I don't see the minister as different [from other professionals] I shouldn't be in this profession. [They've talked to you about this?] They have. The issue of the evening was, "If you have the attitudes you do, why aren't you in medicine or politics or social work rather than the ministry?" (Interview: male, second-year student)

Others question a too traditional approach:

[I hear district committees give people a hard time if they say they are called to the ministry the way other people are called to other occupations.] It depends. Like this guy who's about thirty, that I was talking about before? He's a Fundy [Fundamentalist] and the committee gave him a hard time about that and about him saying that he was called at a certain day and things like that. (Interview: female, first-year student)

Therefore, students learn that the Church is not one when it comes to how ministers should act, but it includes segments and individuals who have different ideas about the appropriate roles and identity of minister.

During field experience, when students work as assistant or associate pastors, they learn that parishioners, too, place conflicting demands on them:

[You say the pastor you're working with thinks you're not fulfilling the role of minister. What about the congregation?] Some have indicated that I don't fit their understanding of a minister. But at the same time, they don't seem to send any negative feelings along with that. It's kind of acceptable. But then again, they're not dependent on me, not calling on me as a quote-unquote "minister"; they've got the full-time pastor for that. If I was the only minister of the church, they might feel differently. I'm more the friend. At times I think they look for both roles, and whether someone can play both roles is my question. (Interview: male, second-year student)

STUDENTS' RESPONSES

The students cannot simply ignore or discount outsiders' discrepant expectations. They intern in churches and must therefore abide by the churches' rules; they must please their examining boards so that they will get jobs later on. Moreover, students come in with very strong traditional notions of their own about how a minister should act and wonder whether a humanistic seminary can actually be the "real thing." Ironically, the humanistic ideology makes it difficult for students to ignore outsiders' traditional expectations because its egalitarian emphasis demands that students care about outsiders' views. The students experience the following paradox: socializers unwittingly communicate the relevance and credibility of traditional expectations by communicating a message (humanism) which holds that recruits take others' (traditional) desires seriously. The problem becomes acute because faculty teach students that all encounters with others are relevant to their future role and should be approached humanistically.

Because the organization makes it difficult for these students to dismiss outsiders' expectations, they take *both* sets of expectations into account and experience an identity problem, wondering what it means to be a minister and how they should act. They find that different audiences expect them not only to do different things ("role conflict") but to be different things. They develop what might be called an ambivalent identity. Students try to meet both the traditional expectations and their teachers' new expectations. They generally adopt a humanistic stance in "public"—in the classroom, in ministry projects, in their leisure pursuits in the seminary, at meals, and so on. Traditional elements of the role show up mostly in private, especially in the in-depth interviews. Students also display role distance from both sets of expectations, moving back and forth between traditional and humanistic roles. They individually and collectively become familiar with, but do not fully adopt, either role.

The Public Humanistic Role

I found evidence for students' acceptance of the humanistic role in their everyday talk. Just as the practical grade-point-average talk of undergraduates reflects the central feature of undergraduate life (Becker et al. 1968), ministry students' talk of "affirming" and "sharing" reflects the humanistic emphasis on personal involvement and equality. One term used often supports the assertion that they regard the minister's role as personal. The word "theologizing," while sometimes used by students to describe a discussion in theology, more often means talking about social problems, public events, or individual experiences in a personal way, whether God is mentioned or not. Some students claim they pick up this term in small group discussions in their first year, when faculty ask them to "reflect on" what is discussed there and write about it. Students, then, often use the word "theologize" to mean "personalize."

Further, students often analyze interpersonal relations, focusing on how they view themselves, particularly in relation to others in the seminary. They believe they must "know" themselves before they can effectively minister to others—and the path to this knowledge is personalized interaction. Respondents express this view when they say that the curriculum constitutes only a small part of the important knowledge of ministry. They define the social skills of interaction (as well as field experience) as the "core knowledge" of ministry. The following response is typical of interviews and ministry projects:

The most important things you learn are outside of class, of course, and if you don't look at seminary as a sort of proving ground for what type of minister you're going to be, then you won't be prepared when you get out. You should look at the [seminary] community around you and say to yourself, "The way I act now and the way I react and the way I relate is going to depend a lot on the kind of person and the kind of minister I'm going to be when I get out of here." I think I pick up at least as much, if not more, out of my community, than I do from my classes. (Interview: male, first-year student)

Ministry students come to expect the faculty to perform a personal role in the classroom, regardless of course content. This becomes clear when faculty violate the expectation:

[Do you think faculty are different here than at other places?] Uh huh, and, in fact, I resent it when they're not. They're almost all ordained pastors besides being scholars, and I resent someone who hasn't integrated those two roles. We've got some professors here whose ordained pastorship doesn't seem to enter into their teaching at all. [Like who?] Professor Mitchell, he bothers me. His language for instance. He uses big words that are cumbersome and unnecessary. [It seems to me there are professors like that in every department.] Yes, but here there should be more of a concern for communication, more human caring. (Interview: male, second-year student)

That students expected their teachers to have personalized interactions in the seminary is also evidenced in the following encounter. There were two women faculty with the same first name, Georgia. I noticed that the students called one of them Georgia-Georgia and referred to the other by her last name, Calhoun. I remarked on this to two women students in the book store:

Maggie said, "Yes, that's significant, we all *respect* Calhoun, but she's not very personal. [Calhoun is also a better-known scholar than the other woman.] I said, "Georgia-Georgia seems to relate her courses more to the ministry than Calhoun." Debbie said, "It's not only that. She's more interested in making her courses relevant to *people*. And Calhoun never comes to any community gatherings. She doesn't come to chapel. That's OK, but even when there's an installation she doesn't come. She didn't even come to the Community dinner! [held once a year for the whole school] And she doesn't come to women's events. It's as if she's above it all." (Field notes)

It is important to note that the student thought it OK that the faculty member did not attend chapel, for this could be seen as an acceptable rejection of a traditional religious event. However, missing a community event was a major transgression.

Students express egalitarian ideas in their ministry projects. In twenty-one of twenty-three papers that I read, ministry students asserted that a relationship of equality should exist between ministers and their congregations. They wrote that ministers should be "enablers," rather than leaders, in the Church; that ministers should attempt to organize participative worship services rather than "carry the show"; and that ministers should seek help from parishioners in accomplishing various tasks. As one student wrote in his project:

Ministry is not a one-way street. It is feedback and response, and, while it may seem that the role definition which society has given us sees us only in the giving position, we must learn to be receivers as well.

These data are compatible with interview data—"I don't like the professional separation between me and the congregation"—and discussions among students.

Students used the humanistic definition of the situation even when other understandings might have been more appropriate. For example, on one occasion I called the operator to get hold of Martha Phillips's (a third-year student) phone number in the city nearby.[1] The operator said there was no Martha Phillips, that there was only a Reverend M. Phillips, which "couldn't be her." I then asked for that number. When I called Martha, I told her what the operator said, primarily to get her reaction to the operator's assumption that a minister couldn't be a woman. I expected Martha, a rather outspoken feminist, to respond to that issue. She did not. Instead, she said in a somewhat defensive tone, "I feel funny about being called Reverend, but I only did that for people in the church or hospitals who would want to get hold of me. That's the only reason I put 'Reverend' in the phone book. I've never asked anyone to call me Reverend."

Students' adoption of the humanistic mode is also shown by the suggestion of one student, and its acceptance by others, that I wear a minsiter's shirt and collar to give me license to "minister" to someone. A nonseminarian dorm dweller, Rita, had recently had an operation, and Jill asked me to come along to visit her. When another student pointed out that visiting hours were over, Jill suggested that we each wear the ministerial collar and shirt in order to get to see Rita. (Having been ordained deacon, Jill had two sets of collars and shirts.) Besides imagining legal repercussions of impersonating a minister, I worried that other students might think this act made a mockery of religious symbols and was going too far. (It was also fairly clear that I could have visited Rita the following day, during visiting hours.) I decided to don the ministerial garb, and Jill and I visited Rita. While some students later chuckled at the story, most thought my behavior appropriate because I was "ministering to someone," and a few thought what I did was not only acceptable but commendable.

The humanistic orientation is antithetical to the "exceptional self-conception" of the minister as one of the select people who

1. I know of only two students who lived in the city rather than on the campus.

receives a calling to become an ordained minister. In twenty-one of twenty-three ministry projects, students wrote that all Christians are called to minister and that the ordained minister's calling is no more special than other occupational callings.

The Private Traditional Role

Students maintain elements of the traditional role of the minister. They discover early on that their peers are neither overly "pious" in their public behavior nor always talking about theology. While most welcome this discovery with relief, they also use it to raise questions about the legitimacy of the organization. Privately, most of them feel that because they are in a seminary, the organization should not tolerate certain behaviors. Although students have different ideas about where the limits should be drawn, they accept the traditional notions of piety that support the impersonal, nonegalitarian role. For example, some think that new ministry students need not be virgins, but that sexual activity in the dorms should be prohibited. Others condone "social drinking" but think it unacceptable for students to get drunk on campus. While most agree that sexuality should be discussed openly, they disagree about whether homosexuals should be admitted to the program or ordained. Some students complained to me about their peers' "bad language," saying that ministers shouldn't swear.

Students who say that their peers are not "religious enough" to become ministers implicitly support the traditional conception of the minister as special by emphasizing the minister's traditional basis of authority. Some students told me that others' religious beliefs were inappropriate for ministers:

[Was seminary what you expected?] No, in some ways. I at least thought everyone here would believe in Christ as Divine, although I knew there would be theological differences. But what I can't understand and what bothered me the most was people who don't even think these questions are *relevant*. I distinguish between social ministry and Christian ministry. Some people here are really into social ministry—they could be psychologists or social workers. They don't see what they're doing as being guided by God or their relationship with God. I can't understand why they're here. (Interview: male, third-year student)

Moreover, while students do not necessarily want to change their behavior, they are well aware of discrepancies between how they act and how others might expect them to act. One student highlighted this discrepancy between expectation and reality by taping the word "monastery" in thick capital letters cut from black paper on the wall over his dorm door. He wanted to suggest that Midwest Seminary is, as he put it, "definitely *not* a monastery." Students sometimes express concern about the imagined responses of Church members to their behavior in the seminary. For example, I was in a dorm room with four female students: two first-year, one second-year, and one third-year student. The third-year student spoke:

And, as I've said, we've been parishioners and we know what we expected the ministers to be like. And we're not like that . . . I mean if the churches knew how we were acting here [referring to drinking some wine, in particular], well . . . (Field notes)

The Calling

That ministry students remain sensitive to traditional expectations is supported by responses to my first question in the open-ended interviews: "How did you get to the seminary?" Twenty-two of the respondents provided lengthy justifications for choosing the ministry. (The rest gave similar justifications later on in the interview.) They made causal connections between people who influenced their decision, autobiographical events, and their present location. Instead of merely *explicating* how they got to the seminary by listing autobiographical events in chronological order, they *warranted* their decision (see Hadden and Lester 1978). Students, it seems, translated my question into another one: "What is your claim to this 'special' identity?" Their interpretation of my question and their answers indicate their sensitivity to the traditional, mystified meaning of the identity. They use the traditional, nonegalitarian language of a "calling" in their warranting talk but quickly qualify their statements to fit humanistic understandings. The following response was common:

I had this teaching job all lined up. It sounds so corny and it's so unlike me, but I kept having this nagging feeling, that every time I decided to do something else I got the feeling "This isn't what you're going to want to do." [What's so corny?] Well, that whole nagging sort of thing, some people would explain it as a call, and I'm not sure I'm willing to define it as that. . . . I wasn't knocked off my horse on the way to Damascus [laughing]. Also, I was being irrational. I've never done this before, but I applied to only one seminary with the rationale that if I was supposed to do this, I would get accepted at the seminary. (Interview: female, third-year student)

This confusion reflects the students' ambivalent attitudes toward the ministerial identity. They try to pull together the discrepant meanings of the identity, with varying degrees of success. While they demystify the "call," and therefore the identity, by saying that it is not a "miraculous event," they maintain its definition as mysterious by contending that "this [seminary] is where they must be."

[What do you mean by call?] Call is wrapped up in your decision to go into whatever you're doing. It's not unique to the ministry. Now my decision was not spontaneous or miraculous. It took a lot of time. It can be spontaneous to some people. . . . When I think of the people I have met up to now, and the experiences I've had, I must come to the conclusion that this is where I should be and what I should be doing. (Interview: male, first-year student)

* * *

I don't feel any more holy as a minister, I don't feel I have anything better or worse than anyone else as far as actual personality, values. I'm still the same person. . . . When I was well on my way to becoming a millionaire, I decided to go into the ministry. [What happened?] On my knees in prayer I couldn't say no any longer. I had been running away. I had everything made, no problems, everything was perfect for me; it was there at the top that I could see I had nothing. I couldn't say no to what I knew back in third grade [when he had first thought of becoming a minister]. And I got a series of confirmations, just bizarre confirmations. I was on my knees, making my decision, thinking "How do I tell my parents?" Then the phone rang and my mom said, "Charles, we were just praying about you and we knew something was going on. What's wrong?" The day before I had made the decision I got a letter from my mother, and at the bottom she wrote, "Your dad thinks you'll goof around for a couple more years, then end up going into the ministry." I got a letter the day after my mom called from my brother in Italy—we write maybe five times a year. He said, "Charles, what in the world are you doing in business, I thought you were going to teach for a few years, then go into the ministry." . . . I was in art for a while, then social work, then teaching, then this business. Then, when I decided on the ministry, suddenly every single experience that I've had I can look back upon and see where it's been a straight road to where I am." (Interview: male, third-year student)

Despite the humanistic rhetoric at Midwest Seminary, "being called" in some form is an important condition for feeling authentic as an aspiring minister. It is so important that some students who were very uncertain about having been called told me they doubted whether they should become ministers:

Part of my hesitancy [about coming to seminary] revolved around not being called to the ministry. I didn't hear God say, "Judy, you've got to be a minister." I just thought that my talents might lie here, and I'd see what would happen. But I was worried that I should have felt something more, you know? (Interview: female, first-year student)

Students who feel they have been called, then, are more convinced that they are the right kind of person for the profession and therefore feel more certain about their decision.

Although the term "calling" is conventionally associated with religious vocations, we expect those we deem professionals to have something akin to a calling. In responding to deprofessionalization, the ministry developed a notion of the calling that established a sense of specialness yet also accommodated modern notions that put their basis of authority into question in the first place. What does the calling look like in this context? Is it possible to establish a sense of specialness as a profession within an egalitarian ideology?

I heard of only one student (who had left before I arrived) who received a calling in the traditional sense. He became part of the students' lore: "He was weird; he left for a more conservative seminary." The students learn in the seminary that being called by God through a vision, at a particular time on a certain day, is not the acceptable way to talk about the calling. Students, however, were well aware of conventional notions of the calling:

Parishioners think that if you weren't struck by a bolt of lightning [she imitated what that might look like] then you somehow can't be as ministerial as if you were. (Interview: female, first-year student)

*   *   *

Well, I guess my call was long-distance, as they say [laughing]. (Class field notes: male, first-year student)

*   *   *

Now being called doesn't mean God taps you on the shoulder; the calling can be interpreted in different ways. (Interview: female, third-year student)

How is the call talked about? One popular notion is "We are all called to minister." One student put it succinctly:

Ministry is not just something done by pastors, preachers, chaplains, or pastoral psychologists. Ministry is a very inclusive term. . . . We are all called to minister. (Interview: female, second-year student)

Another student said:

I have a very strong sense of lay people doing ministry, and that all Christians are called to be ministers in some way. . . . I was doing lay ministry at a chapel [before coming to seminary] though I didn't have that definition of it at the time. I still had the conception that the minister was someone who headed the congregation. That's not a very biblical way to look at the ministry. I've learned this here and I've grown out of that very narrow understanding. (Interview: female, second-year student)

On the face of it, the idea that all are called to minister suggests that the ministry is neither distinctive nor better than other "callings." However, the quotation above also implies that the ministry —rather, ministering—is the all-important activity in this world. This is no minor point in an age when the traditional basis of religious authority has been undermined. The ministry becomes the vocation whose perspective informs all work and which forms the basis of comparison for other occupations. Anything one does becomes, by the students' definition, a matter of ministering. Further, the new ideology emphasizes that people minister in different ways, which implies that although the ordained ministry is merely one form of ministry, it nevertheless has its own niche. It is ordained ministers who presumably provide the perspective and ideals which others may "equally" follow. Hence, "new" ministers are able to establish the sense that the ministry is special, even given an egalitarian ideology.

Although the idea is that all are called to minister, some students only mention other *professions* when they talk about the calling. They establish specialness in a seemingly nonelitist way by saying their calling "is no more special than a doctor's calling." They are, at the same time, placing themselves in the high-status category of accepted professionals:

It [the ministry] means something special to me. I don't mean to sound like ministers are better than anyone else. If I had wanted to be a dentist and became a dentist, that would be something special to me. But I wanted to become a minister, and I became one and I very much treasure that. (Interview: female, third-year student)

*   *   *

I think people have a general calling, to achieve some meaning or understanding of life, to understand what their strengths and weaknesses are,
to develop their livelihood around those. I feel I have a social responsibility to help others. The way people live out their calling is basically of their
own choice, or their own understanding of what education they have,
what they may like to do. Some achieve it as teachers, some as doctors,
some as lawyers. Oh, some as ministers [laughing]. (Interview: male,
second-year student)

In discussing the ministry as something "everyone is called to do,"
the students sometimes explicitly included low-status occupations
in their talk.

I really feel more called to be a Christian than to be anything else. Professional ministry is just my way of being a Christian. I don't think that my
call is any more grand or important than the call the janitor gets. I'm
called to be a Christian, to deal with life in the eyes of faith. The call to be
a pastor has come because of who I am and my gifts and talents. (Interview: male, second-year student)

In a seminar, the students were discussing the role of the minister. One student said:

"Last summer I was driving a bus and, from listening to people and talking to people, I sensed that people are hungry for community. I think it's
a good time to be a minister." Everyone nodded. Another student said,
"And this ministering may even happen while driving a bus." The first
student said, "Hey, wait, I don't want to drive a bus. I'm not so sure ministering goes on there." The second student said, "Sure it does. You can
minister while driving a bus!" The six others in the seminar agreed with
the second student and criticized the first one rather strongly for sounding elitist. (Field notes)

Since people generally do not think of low-status workers as
having callings, but jobs, will including them in the general category "calling" lower the status of the ordained minister? What
seems to be going on here is the establishment of the ministry as
special by upgrading lower-status occupations (rather than down-
grading the ordained ministry through association with low-
status work). This is an interesting way to talk about one's own
work as special without sounding elitist. From the ministers' view,
the "religious" perspective provided by the ordained ministry becomes the overridingly important one, but even low-status occu-

pations may share the professional prestige. The ministers establish specialness, one might say, through magnanimity.

The key to establishing specialness within an egalitarian ideology in the ministry is to use religious terms in ways that do not make the occupation sound elitist. Some students learn how to do this better than others. For example, in the following case, the student has learned to dissociate himself from the traditional notion of the calling, but has not also learned to use religious terminology without sounding—to himself—elitist:

The calling is in how you interpret it. I'm called in that I feel I know what I'm supposed to be doing. I didn't get a letter [laughing] or a booming voice—lightning. I'm not really into getting messages or visions or whatever. [I've heard some district committees give people a hard time if they talk about the calling in certain ways.] Well, maybe those people didn't put it in theological terms. I wouldn't go up to the committee and say Joe Blow has a calling to be a janitor in that building and my call is the same thing as that. [Do you think it's the same thing, or you just wouldn't say that to them?] Well, I wouldn't say that to them. But, well, I think there's a bit more to it [ministering] than that. [He talked more slowly and began to fidget.] Gee, that's an elitist kind of thing to say—Well, it's special in that you're given certain responsibilities that others can't do. [Like other jobs?] Well, hey, gee, I've really backed myself into a corner here. For instance, when a person's ordained, you want to call it a gift? They're ordained to preach, to administer the sacraments. Alright, let me go out on a limb—ordination is a laying on of hands. (Interview: male, second-year student)

This student, by not including low-status jobs as simply one form of ministering, finds that he can only establish the specialness of the ordained ministry by invoking the exclusive, traditional basis of authority. He recognizes, however, that this will not do, for it contradicts the egalitarian ideology. In the context of the seminary he is indeed going out on a limb in characterizing the distinctiveness of the ministry through the laying on of hands.

Ironically, those who accept the humanistic understanding of the ministerial calling can also use it to exit from the seminary. If one can minister to others by "doing anything," one might very well do something else. One can, after all, minister in some other way. As we will see in chapter 6, female students, in particular, used this definition of calling to justify exiting from an occupation which could pose problems for their interpersonal lives later on.

IMPLICATIONS

The conventional definition of profession is a group of people who know what is best for their clients. It also means that professionals, not clients, should determine the norms of professional behavior. Without this implicit notion of superiority, the meaning of professional becomes problematic. We can see this occurring at Midwest Seminary. Students develop problems of professional identification not only because they receive discrepant expectations from insiders and outsiders; the humanistic message itself, by making clients' views central, contradicts the core meaning of professionalism and renders it ambiguous.

In most professional programs, students might experience a different dilemma of professional identification. In conventional programs, socializers simply will not allow their students to see themselves as professionals. In medical school, for instance, faculty treat students as boys and girls rather than as budding professionals (Becker et al. 1961). That doctors are esteemed and doing esoteric work is clear to students. Consequently, medical students do not develop the same problems of identification that the ministry students do. They do, however, have the problem of being denied an early introduction to medical responsibilities and identification with medicine.

At Midwest Seminary, socializing agents and outsiders treat students as professionals from the beginning. Ironically, neophytes develop dilemmas of professional identification in this situation. This occurs because the humanistic professional role is only partly "professional." The distinctiveness of the professional role is unclear and the authority of the profession questionable. Students have little with which to identify.

4

Humanistic Religion

Humanistic religion is grounded in the human situation rather than in the transcendent. In this view, the distinction between transcendent and mundane realities no longer exists, for everyday reality takes on a religious significance. Hence, humanistic religion has a this-worldly emphasis. Religion becomes a matter of human symbolism rather than a God-given truth (Gilkey 1967).

A conception of religion as symbolic, situated in time and place, and of this world suggests that religiosity is relative. Religion becomes subjective, individualized, and privatized (Lemert 1974a, 1974b; Luckmann 1967; Miller 1975). Consequently, ministers no longer set the standards for or enforce moral purity and orthodoxy (Bellah 1964). Rather, individuals become responsible, more than the Church, for their religiosity and even for determining what religious behavior is (Hiller 1969, 183). The Church simply provides an environment for the individual's spiritual growth and ministers become enablers rather than truth givers or standard setters. Consequently, the faculty at Midwest Seminary do not expect the students to be devoted to traditionally religious duties or to serve as traditional moral exemplars in the community. In addition, the subjectivizing of religion has led to a bias against intellectualizing and an emphasis on "feeling-talk."

49

WORLD-OPENNESS

In the new theology, "liberation is obtained from rigid and closed worldviews, and the world is accepted as sanctioned ground for action" (Hiller 1969, 80). The less rigid and closed world view tends to be associated with less rigid standards for conventional ministerial behavior. As the world becomes an open place for religiosity, ministers can participate in many activities once considered off limits for them.

Instructional personnel at Midwest Seminary do not advocate partying, smoking, drinking, and swearing, but neither do they say that such behaviors are bad. Within the humanistic framework, these behaviors become matters students should deal with themselves and do not determine whether they will become good ministers. Students discover this view when they note that the organization does not interfere in their leisure activities. Student dorm life, including parties, are not monitored by the school. Further, faculty sometimes say that behavior people usually think of as routine deviance for most people, but "real" deviance for religious people, is not necessarily bad. For example, in a class called "The Changing Conception of the Church's Self-Image" (the course title itself indicates the new orientation), the following interchange occurred:

The professor said, "When I was younger I saw someone smoking after a revival meeting. At that time I thought that anyone who smoked or drank was a sinner. When I saw this person smoking, I thought, 'Oh, the revival didn't work.' A male, second-year student said, "Yeah, it didn't take." The class laughed. The professor said, "We are *all* born into the Body of Christ, yet we set up standards for who should be let in and let out." (Field notes)

The professor implies that he used to think smoking indicated the absence of religiosity but now he knows better.

Just as the faculty do not equate abstaining from deviant activities as good, they do not emphasize participating in traditionally pious activities as the way to self-betterment. The organization institutionalizes few conventionally religious activities. One of them, a half-hour chapel service, is held twice a week. But even participation in chapel is officially and informally defined as optional.

My observations indicate that the high point of chapel service for students and others is the sociability of the reception following the service. Here, students, faculty, administrators, and staff chat, drink coffee, and eat doughnuts for about fifteen minutes.

Faculty sometimes show role distance from traditional expectations of piety and respect for conventional religion in their classes. They usually do this through their jokes:

I went with Jean over to Assessment Services. Jean said to the secretary, "I signed up for assessment last year but I couldn't take it. So I'd like to sign up again." One of the seminary faculty standing nearby said, smiling, "Isn't there some penalty for that? Hmm, well, say 5,000 Hail Mary's." The three of us laughed. After we left, Jean decided to fill the form out right away and hand it in. She told me later, "When I handed it in, Anderson was still there. I told him it would be a good idea to hand in the form right away. He said, 'That's intelligent. Take off some Hail Mary's.'" (Field notes)

* * *

In a class on pastoral psychotherapy the instructor was discussing a "case." He then said, "I asked the client who her heroes are, maybe I should ask *you* [the class]." He then suddenly did an imitation of Christ on the Cross. Some of the class laughed nervously, others just laughed. He said, "Some of you seemed shocked at that." The third-year, male student sitting next to me smiled and said, "Only the first-years." (Field notes)

* * *

In a time-management seminar, the class was divided into groups of three in which they discussed problems with their schedules. One group said their problem was having self-expectations that were too high. Someone in the class responded, "Yes, if it hurts it must be good." The instructor said, "Oh, the joy of suffering. Jesus did it, so can I." The class laughed. (Field notes)

Because faculty fail to emphasize the religious in the traditional sense but do emphasize that ministers should be egalitarian—ministers are, after all, only human—students get the idea that people who show their religiosity are using it to establish a sense of superiority and are therefore acting inappropriately. Since the conventional ministerial role is that of a superordinate, demystifying the role involves getting rid of the signs and displays of religious specialness, such as robes, the collar, talk about God, and pious behaviors. (Hence, the students had allowed me to wear traditional garb as a means to a humanistic end.) In a dorm room in which three female students were present, the following interchange took place:

One student said, "I ran into this guy I used to know, who's Fundamentalist. Anyway, he took some of us out to lunch, to McDonald's. And you know what he said? He said, 'Let's pray.'" The other student said, "Oh, gross!" I said, "What's so gross about it?" The first student said, "It's too public, it looks like he was trying to tell everyone that he's pious. It's as if he's saying, 'I'm pious, why can't you be?' It's like saying he's superior." The other students nodded in agreement. (Field notes)

Students might have challenged this man's behavior primarily on the basis of its inappropriateness for the setting—McDonald's. The fact that they challenged him on the basis of his lack of humanism is evidence for the strength of their humanistic beliefs.

The demystification of "religious people" was made explicit in the following interview with a member of the faculty.

It's in preaching that people see their prejudices, their hangups, it's a personal thing. Now some preachers don't see it that way. They gloss over what attitudes they're showing by saying "It's the Word of God." I don't see it that way. I make the students hear and see what they're saying. That's why I use the videotape. . . . One student whose sermon I was commenting on yesterday started off the sermon by saying "There's a story about a boy who . . ." I told him it sounded like the boy was *him*—you know, the classic case of "I have a *friend* with a problem, and it's *you*." So I told him that either he should *say* the story's about him and be open about his problem; or, if the person's problem is too intense or personal for the pulpit, then leave it out entirely. But why should he leave it open, why leave me with that curiosity? If it's a problem he can talk about then he *should*, because it's good for the congregation to see that even people into religion have problems.

In the lounge one evening, a former student of the seminary who had returned for a visit was speaking with one first-year female student and one second-year male student:

The returning student said, "What would you say the students are like here, pious or what?" The first-year female student said, "We're not pious at all." The former student replied, "That's good. Three years ago, we had some of those holy people around, who really could not relate to the real world. They went around like, 'I'm Christian, I'm holy, I'm happy.' They were all clean-shaven, short hair, conservative dress. I'm glad there have been some changes." The second-year student said, "The problem is we're not concerned with being pious at all." The female student said in a sarcastic tone, "Well, listen to him—*pious*." The second-year student replied, "I know. To you pious has a negative connotation. You think it means holier-than-thou. . . . It's as if there's an understanding that you shouldn't talk about faith here. It's understood." (Field notes)

Given humanistic notions of religion, it is understandable that students did not treat me as an outsider. In their view, even a Jewish agnostic can become part of the minister's religious experience, for almost everything and everyone is defined as part of God's reality. For example, a student I had interviewed a few days earlier came to my room and said to me:

Remember in my interview I said that I felt I had to be called to be a minister? And I've been called, I *know*, to be here *this year*, I've been called to consider the ministry. But I don't know if I've been called to be ordained. [Well, I don't think I'm qualified to . . . um] God's will is communicated through *people*, so by talking to *you*, for instance, it may help me to find God's guidance. (Field notes)

Indeed, with an understanding of religion and ministering as interpersonal and all-inclusive, some students who thought I was a good listener suggested I become a minister.

ANTI-INTELLECTUALISM

Most of the faculty emphasize the heart of ministry as interpersonal rather than intellectual. Intellectualizing did go on in class, but it was often treated as secondary or deprecated. For example, during the break period in a small theology seminar which had had an intellectual-personal mix, one of the students asked the instructor a question about something he had written on the blackboard. The instructor looked a little embarrassed and said in an apologetic tone, "Yes, I like to keep up my image, that I'm a theological thinker." The instructor expressed role distance from the image of the "cold thinker," presumably evidenced by his having written some theological terms on the blackboard! In another class, another professor said, smiling, "Since I guess most of you expect a course on theology to talk about God, the next two sessions will be it." He then went on to emphasize the "experiential" as the most important part of theology. In still another class, a professor was making the point that students should refrain from using big words the congregation might not understand. He mentioned a cartoon in which the minister is speaking to a snoring congregation. He said the caption read, "Look, I know you're thinking Sabelleus, but . . . ," indicating that the minister was insensitive to the congregation's boredom at hearing an intellectual sermon.

Consequently, students believe that those few peers who engage in intellectual talk are arrogant (and therefore bad) or are defensive and need therapy. Students who tried to discuss theology in the cafeteria, for instance, made people noticeably uncomfortable and were often resented by their peers. One third-year student who attempted to intellectualize matters also recognized that by doing so he could bring out theological divisions among the students that would otherwise be left unstated:

There's a lot of unspoken tension about faith issues . . . I mean some people should really be erupting at each other! If they knew how different they really are they should be asking, "How can we both be here and should we both be here?" And they should talk about these things, but they don't. (Interview)

This student was atypical. Most learn to refrain from intellectualizing or come to believe it is bad. For example, one student wrote the following in his ministry project:

As I enlarge my world view, I also have found that I must look inward toward a better self-understanding. With the help of Assessment Services and new friendships, I have been made aware of the areas where I personally need to grow. I tend to intellectualize my way through emotional situations which I seem to set up for myself. . . . I use overpowerful language in order to get my point across and to break communication barriers which often should be handled more carefully. I let the debator in me come through.

In his ministry project, another student put it:

In ministry we must give up the security of a system of verbal, intellectual formulations and enter into human relationships through love and trust.

After about three weeks in the field, I remarked to a few students that I had yet to hear a theological discussion. In response to that remark, students would now and then call me over if they were discussing anything remotely intellectual, saying things like "Quick, Sherryl, we're having a theological discussion," or "Let's have a theological discussion for Sherryl." They were making fun of my expectation that a seminary would be pervaded by religious talk. Also, they sometimes used jokes to stop others from intellectualizing. For example, at breakfast one morning, a first-year student was discussing Zimbardo's well-known prison experiment, relating it to questions of human nature. Two other students continued to eat their breakfast, but didn't participate in the conversation. After about ten minutes, one of them got up to leave. She said, mocking an upper-class British accent, "Well, thank you for this theological, spiritual, intellectual discussion." The other student chuckled.

Because of the new definition of religious people as "normal," or "like everyone else," students come to reject their earlier expectation that a seminary should be characterized by conventional religious behavior and theological talk:

I thought that everyone else here who came to ministry would be concerned only with religion. This is absurd, as absurd as thinking that when I was in music I would think only about music, or that you, in sociology, would be concerned only with sociology. Why I didn't grasp that before I came, I don't know. I wouldn't expect people in journalism, say, to only talk about journalism. But people expect that with religion, *even* people who come here to study. (Interview, female, first-year student)

A third-year student who had just returned from an intern year said in an interview:

I expected the dinner table talk to be theologically oriented, you know, "Well, did you study Martin Luther's 95 Theses today?" And to show you how much my mind has changed on these things, well, last week I was sitting, talking to Beth [another third-year woman] across the table [in the cafeteria]. There were two guys sitting next to us—first-year students—and they were into a deep theological discussion, kind of like what I imagined would go on long ago. We just kind of looked at them and said to each other later, "Gee, I wonder how long it's going to take them to get out of *that*?" [laughing]. (Field notes)

SOCIALIZATION PROBLEMS

Students initially have strong conventional expectations of religiosity, both ideologically and behaviorally. They enter the seminary expecting their peers and teachers to act in religious ways. In short, students expect an institution of religion to be a religious institution. Many of them talked about what they thought they would have to give up in seminary (partying, dancing, smoking, drinking, swearing) and what they thought they would have to do (daily devotions, talk about God, prayer groups).

I went out for dessert with four female students. After about fifteen minutes of joking around, Donna said, "Gee, I wish we could have done this last year, before coming here, than I wouldn't have worried about coming." Belle said, "You mean going out with seminary students before we became seminary students?" Donna said, "Yes. I remember talking to Nancy about that last quarter. It turns out we were both worried, before we got here, that there wouldn't be any fun people at seminary." Belle said, laughing, "Oh, but you should have realized that *you're* fun, and you're going to seminary, so there must be others—I know what you mean; I wondered about that, too." (Field notes)

It is quite common in occupational socialization settings that students' initial expectations are incorrect. In the case of the ministry, however, the students' experience is one of reality shock, for the realities of seminary life are not just different but the opposite of what they expected. For example, what was previously defined as deviant behavior (drinking, smoking, swearing) isn't, now, and what was once defined as religious behavior (piety) is now defined as deviant.

The students are in fact ambivalent about their initial conventional expectations of religiosity; they want to become ministers, but fear the "monastic" life. Their ambivalence perhaps paralleled mine. As a field worker in a seminary, I expected and was willing to make certain sacrifices, such as suspending skepticism about religion, becoming more polite, going to chapel, being proselytized, and altering other acts or attitudes. Students and I also reacted similarly to the lack of religiosity—some relief at having our tasks made easier mixed with an uneasy feeling about the legitimacy of the organization. They wonder: "Can an unconventional seminary really be a seminary?"

STUDENTS' RESPONSES

Students largely accept the redefinition of religious deviance, acting "publicly" against traditional expectations and notions of religiosity, often through cynical remarks and jokes. Entering the seminary with traditional expectations, I, like many new recruits, was surprised at ministry students' lack of "pious" behavior. I was equally struck by the prevalence of jokes with religious content, such as making a pun on "saving a chair" for someone (and asking the chair to repent) or calling poor typing "typing in tongues." Students often point out discrepancies between their behavior and outsiders' expectations of them, saying things like, "You wouldn't know this is a seminary, right?" In light of the dominant humanistic expectations in the seminary, and the intensity of traditional expectations on the outside, this joking behavior is less surprising. Students are enacting collective role distance from traditional expectations. The behavior seems to say "We do not assume the traditional role which you outsiders are giving us." The students, like the faculty, made jokes and cynical remarks about religion among themselves.

In the evening, one male student, three female students, and I were in one of the women's rooms. There was a lull in the conversation. One of the women was leaning on the towel rack that was nailed to the closet. Suddenly the rack fell, which startled us a bit. The woman who had been leaning on it said, "Oh, it's the Holy Spirit! Wait, the Devil made me do it." We laughed. (Field notes)

After having arrived late to the party in the dorm, one of the first-year women said to me:

It's too bad you weren't here earlier. [What happened?] Oh, some of the guys were doing a mock Communion, doing it all wrong. They used pretzels. It was really funny. (Field notes)

Students often made fun of outsiders' traditional expectations of ministers. For example, the following exchange I had with a second-year student alludes to parishioners' views of ministers as asexual:

I was in Agnes' room. She said, "Do you mind if I change in front of you?" I said, "No." She said, "You can put it in your study—ministers *do* have breasts." (Field notes)

The students learn that becoming a minister at Midwest Seminary means they should act counter to traditional expectations. For example, one of the new students expressed some concern about taking the vocational tests required of all members of the first-year cohort:

At breakfast Peter, the new student, said nervously, "Well, I'm off to be vocationally tested, to see that I'm not fit to be a minister." The two other second-year male students laughed. One of them said, "And that you *should* be here." (Field notes)

The new student was worried about not presenting himself as a traditional minister on the test. The veteran is telling him that he will fit in at the seminary to the extent that he doesn't fit the traditional image.

Although most of the jokes made fun of traditional religion, some of them also revealed students' skepticism about whether a humanistic seminary could really be a seminary. Some jokes suggested that the student was questioning the legitimacy of an organization that calls itself a seminary but doesn't seem religious. The students could accept their peer's remarks because they ostensibly made fun of traditional religion. But the joke may have carried another message; it also mocked the lack of religiosity. Students could question the lack of religiosity and make fun of parishioners' "misguided" expectations at the same time:

A male seminary student walked into the cafeteria at lunch and neared our table. Ron, a first-year student, said to him, "Hi, Father. How are you doing?" The student he called Father said, "Fine, fine." I said to Ron, pretending to whisper, "Hmm, how come he's called Father?" Ron said, "Oh, I coined that because he's going to switch to an Anglican seminary and their priests are called Father. Also [smiling], he's High Church." I said, "I don't fully understand what that is." Ron said, "Oh, the service is full of liturgies, chants and praying—really structured: Not like here." I said, "You'd say this is Low Church?" Ron said, "Yeah." Eric, another first-year student, said smiling, "No. Basement Church." We laughed. (Field notes)

The notion of "Basement Church" could be interpreted as fairly insulting, hinting that the seminary goes too far in its rejection of traditional religion. To provide more of a context, my interview with Eric and other observational data suggest that he is quite traditional. Eric is the student quoted in chapter 3 who couldn't understand why students who "don't see what they're doing as being guided by God or their relationship with God" would enter a seminary. However, because Eric's joke, on the surface, put down High Church, the students found the joke acceptable.

In my interview a few months later with the student called Fa-

ther, he said, "My impression is that the school is about half liberal and half conservative. Yeah, half conservative and half . . .
heretic. Yes," he said, laughing, "half heretic." He then classified
himself in the heretic category. The notion of heretic is not a
humanistic, but a traditional word. Although this student dis-
paraged the conservatives, his definition of the others as heretics
suggests at least a slight put-down of those who are less conservative. Perhaps he used this strong language to show that he is not,
as his High Church affiliation indicates to his peers, traditional.
When I asked him in an interview about the High Church/Low
Church distinction, he characterized his affiliation with the former as a preference or taste, rather than a matter of being essentially traditional.

[What do people not like about High Church services?] Vestments, para-
phernalia, the formalness. I do it because I like it. There's more of a cele-
bration type atmosphere to it. Face it. We do things because we like to.
And then we come up with some superstructure to back it up. And people are uncomfortable with that.

"Father," however, was not the only person who used the term
"heretic" in a joking context to characterize many of the students.
Other students also used the term "apostate" to describe themselves and their peers.

After two weeks in their first quarter of study, a few of the new
students talked about their preconceptions of seminaries over
lunch in the cafeteria:

Others had left the cafeteria. Martin and I stayed to talk. He said, "You
know what I worried the most about in coming here? What my roommate would be like. I figured I could get a really weird roommate in a
seminary. I worried that I wouldn't be able to drink beer with him, in
front of him. And my first night here, he not only brought in a case, but
the *best*—Heineken. I'm not sure what to make of that! (Field notes)

Martin was laughing as he said this, but also fidgeted and looked a
bit confused. Although questioning the legitimacy of the organization on the basis of the kind of beer students drink rather than
the fact that they drink at all may seem ridiculous to an outsider,
Martin is experiencing the dilemma which most students never resolve: which behavior and attitudes are definitely not "religious"
and which are acceptable? Humanism does not provide the an-

swers, partly because the new order lacks moral exemplars. But in a context in which clients expect moral exemplars, to refrain from defining "the good" (except for self-disclosure, which is open to anyone) is not enough. As we will see in the next chapter, this becomes particularly troublesome because socializers leave the question of goodness open but also lead students to expect homogeneity of "goodness" among their peers and teachers.

Students also joked and made cynical remarks about the humanistic role, and particularly the humanistic vocabulary, on occasion. For example, I was in Ellen's room (Ellen is a first-year student). Phil, a second-year student, came over. They were talking rather sarcastically about the argot of seminary students, such as "affirming" and "sharing." Ellen spoke, "Another big one is 'community.'" Phil replied, "Yes, and that means everyone knows your business." Because humanistic expectations predominate in the seminary, students made such remarks more often in small groups of close friends and outside the classroom than in large groups. Moreover, in the company of close friends, students sometimes used traditional standards to evaluate others.

Students, then, dealt with their ambivalence about humanistic religion by expressing some of those feelings in jokes with double meanings. Also, although seldom in public, students did talk and think about their faith, whether they had been called to the ministry, and their conceptions of God. However, they tended to keep these matters to themselves or discussed them in private settings with a close friend or two or with me:

I was waiting for a phone call in the dorm hallway. I heard two students talking in the room across from the phone. One of the women left. I said, "Gee, I thought I heard the word theology in there." Kathy said, "Yes, it does happen sometimes. You have to look hard for it, though. But sometimes during the noise at lunch two people will be off in a corner discussing . . . Tillich. Or in someone's room like this, it will be going on." (Field notes)

Some students who were quite adept at making religious jokes seemed to transform in the interview situation, suddenly showing a hidden, serious, religious side. Although I do not have distributions on how many people prayed privately, I do know that some fourteen students did, alone or with a friend. However, the norms prohibiting the public display of a serious attitude toward religion often made it difficult for them to find a prayer partner:

I had to grope a lot the first term as to praying with other persons, I mean knowing which persons would be into that sort of thing and which wouldn't. [How did you go about finding out?] Well, I was in a class last term called "Theology of Prayer." Susan was in that, so we started praying together. . . . We talked and theologized more about prayer in that class than doing it, so you could find out how people felt about it. (Interview: female, first-year student)

It is likely that more students wanted someone to pray with than looked for one. My data suggest that a situation of pluralistic ignorance may have existed: students wished at times to be "religious" with their peers but feared that they would disapprove.

IMPLICATIONS

The esteem accorded professional knowledge in a society is partly sustained by the profession's definition of it as esoteric, either technically, intellectually, or both. As a way of establishing their turf and excluding clients from decision making, professions usually develop sets of terms, or jargon, which only those who have had the training can understand.

Religious terminology, like any professional language, can be understood only by those who learn it. In the seminary, students do learn certain terms in their theology classes that outsiders probably would not understand. But, this humanistic program's client-centered emphasis downplays the importance of theological terms. Hence, technical terminology and intellectual talks about theology rarely occur in students' conversations or even in their class discussions. In fact, professors who write books and articles on theology express their distance from the scholarly role when interacting with students.

Students at Midwest Seminary do learn an argot—that of psychologizing. Although not all outside audiences understand this, it is characteristically close to the contemporary language of everyday life. The language is more expressive than many parishioners might like, but it is nevertheless easier for them to comprehend than such terms as "hermeneutics." That is the problem; the language is so common that it does not distinguish religious knowledge from everyday information and talk. As a common language, it fails to provide a sense that the ministry is distinctive and esteemed.

This implies that traditional professional languages legitimate professional authority to students in other schools, keeping them from developing dilemmas of professional identification. Without having a clear sense of the function, knowledge, and tasks of their profession, students may have problems identifying with it. Lacking a vocabulary of motives, they may also have trouble developing professional commitment.

5

The Rhetoric of Community

Rhetoric is a means to change others' attitudes, beliefs, or behaviors. Those who challenged the knowledge base and the esteem of the ministry left the clergy with a problem: How could the clergy convince others that theirs is a distinctive and esteemed occupation?

The ministry developed a rhetoric of community. The term "community" connotes specialness because it confers group identity; in modern times, to call a group a community is to suggest that it has something distinctive and valued to offer. The rhetoric suggests that the ministry is a special and esteemed body—a professional community. The term does not suggest what distinguishes the ministry from other occupations, but its rhetorical value lies in its ambiguity. Since the relegitimation of the ministry involved a secularizing of their tradition—making religion personal, egalitarian, and historically grounded—defining the community too closely might make it more apparent that ministerial services are similar to what other "therapeutic" occupations offer. In addition, the word also has traditional appeal, for "community" has always been used in the rhetoric of religion.

At the seminary, socializers used the word as means of social control, that is, to convince recruits to do the things designed to make them good ministers, such as disclosing personal information to their teachers and peers. Students need to be convinced

63

because they, like most people, are accustomed to choosing the people they will reveal themselves to. Socializers used "community" to suggest that they and their charges were united. This unity presumably derives from their professional reference group—the ministry. In short, socializers used community to identify their interests with recruits so that recruits would trust them. Students then learned to do certain things as part of their obligations as community members. Given conventional understandings of a community as a close-knit group, "community" was a particularly appropriate rhetoric; it justified the collective sharing of personal information and feelings in a conventionally nonintimate setting.

In this context, "community" is essentially defined by the expectation and experience of identification and good feelings, not by the content of the beliefs members presumably share. Community becomes a high-level abstraction which may mean all things to all people—faculty and administrators use it ambiguously and variously.

THE MEANINGS OF COMMUNITY

When they arrive at the seminary, new candidates discover that the rhetoric of community is popular among instructional personnel and students. People used the word so often that I noted its salience in my field notes after only a few days. For example, in my first week, students used it at meals, a women's caucus meeting, a discussion group on homosexuality, three chats in the hallway, two interviews, and an informal gathering in a student's room. Upon further inspection, I noticed that it was part of the "official" rhetoric as well, appearing in the school catalog and in orientation speeches and sermons given by the faculty and administrators. Faculty, staff, and students referred to the organization as "the Community" in a taken-for-granted way in their everyday talk.

A rhetoric often includes words that are synonymous with what sociologists call values, such as truth, freedom, "the good." People can use these abstractions to mean many things, thereby giving them many referents. For example, at Midwest Seminary, people used "community" to refer to feelings ("sense of community"), but also to forms of social organization or levels of community (such as the school, friendship groups, or another person) and to activities (partying, praying, or revealing personal information to one or several persons). Instructional personnel used the word in diverse ways, and some explicitly encouraged students to do the same. For example, in a theology class, the professor said:

Church is not community. Community is different from the parish, it's an *event*. The pastor is there to make the event of community possible in the church. Also, there are different communities. Like yesterday, I heard some good news and I called up five or six people, related the news to them, and they were there for me. These are friends I can share the good news with, one of my support groups. And there are many support networks. (Field notes)

At Midwest Seminary, some students mainly associate community with traditional notions of spiritual communion or *koinonia* (being part of the Body of Christ). This meaning of community usually became clear when a student felt it was absent:

I wonder sometimes, where is community? Where are the people who are supposed to be One in the Body of Christ? (Field notes: male, third-year student)

* * *

I just thought of something else about what my expectations were [about coming to the seminary]. Well, one thing was the sense of spirituality or community about Midwest Seminary. I expected there to be more togetherness at times. [Doing what kinds of things?] Well, like going to chapel on Tuesday and Thursday. (Interview: female, first-year student)

Others emphasize community as a matter of interpersonal relations, expecting it to result from "talks," not from traditional worship:

I'm better now at talking with people, because of the community. I've been able to open up more here. And people listen. That sense of community, this is so different from a school where you go to class and you go home and you can put aside your study. To me, here, it's your living: it's a totality. (Interview: female, first-year student)

Others equate community with alternative lifestyles or political activism:

Melanie, a third-year student, said, "I don't think there's as much community here as there used to be. You think so, Alice?" Alice, another third-year student, said, "I think you're right." Melanie continued, "The students this year don't seem to be doing the crazy things that students did in the past; there seems to be less community and more conservatism." I asked, "What kinds of things?" Melanie replied, "Oh, beer bashes and parties. And people were into, at least interested in, alternatives to the Church. We had a lot of discussions about questioning the Church. We went into the community." Rhonda, another third-year student, said, "Yes, social gospel." (Field notes)

The following student used community in a spiritual and political context:

I want to build a community of faith that is concerned with social issues and tries to unite people, to bring people into a covenant of mutual caring and understanding. (Interview: male, first-year student)

Still others associate it with social activities organized by various groups in the seminary:

I went to my mailbox around noon. William, a third-year student, said to me, "This is a good place. You chose a good place to study. I was at another seminary before, out East, and there wasn't much of a sense of community there at all. People kind of went their own way. . . . Here I think the institution creates community. Like the women and the black groups, they make events and things, events for everyone to go to." I said, "So you think of community in terms of happenings in the seminary?" William said, "Not only that, though I think that's what helps it happen. It's a general feeling of being part of a group. The events make you feel that way." (Field notes)

Because everyone used the same word, community, and valued it, students presumed that others' usages coincided with theirs. Instructional personnel, then, created a situation of false consensus by using the humanistic rhetoric (Scheff 1970). Specifically, they led students to believe that they shared an understanding of the language, even when they did not. One of the reasons this situation could develop was because the words fit into several popular ideologies. Because recruits enter the seminary with traditional expectations of ministers, faculty's use of a rhetoric that fits both humanism and traditionalism may help gain students' trust and get them to cooperate in the measures designed to change them. The wide appeal of such an ambiguous but valued term as community was seductive to most students.

By emphasizing any abstract word that people value, socializers may produce a situation of false consensus and get recruits to trust them. Using the word "community," however, increases the likelihood, because people today typically associate the word with identification. It indicates people "like oneself," people one can trust (Gusfield 1975). Further, through their previous participation in fellowship groups and churches, these students had come to expect a spirit of community at the seminary. The expectation of community is an expectation of identification; students expect to like, to be like, and to be liked by, their peers and teachers.

SOCIALIZATION PROBLEMS: DISCREPANCIES BETWEEN IDEALS AND REALITY

Homogeneity

The seminary students learn to use "community" in many ways, but at the same time they learn to expect similarities between their teachers and themselves. Evidence of like-mindedness is important to them because it convinces them that the ministry is a special and distinctive occupational group—a "real" profession. The ambiguity of the term initially makes it likely that the students will think they are united and homogeneous, but they are also likely to discover real heterogeneity among themselves and their teachers.

The word "community" does not specify which types of homogeneity legitimize membership. Because the program does not present a finite set of meanings of community and encourages students to develop their own, they often have different notions about how they expect their peers and teachers to be like them. Some students expect their peers to share their theological views, while others think that consensus on matters of routine deviance, such as smoking, drinking, and sexual activity, is imperative. Students' varied expectations became clear when others violated them:

The people here, some of them say they're called to the ministry but they don't have a personal relationship with Christ. I haven't confronted them, but I feel like asking, "What are you going to do when someone comes in looking for Christ, and you haven't even found him yourself?" (Interview: male, first-year student)

* * *

I don't know *why*, but I expected people to be more devout. [What do you mean?] Well, I guess I expected the women to be virgins. Wait, I guess I didn't expect them all to be virgins, but I didn't expect people here to be sexually active. (Interview: female, first-year student)

Because socializers use the rhetoric of community so much, students may feel they have been cheated if their peers are not like them in the ways they expected. They may then wonder about the legitimacy of the seminary's demands, for it is the faculty's use of the rhetoric which makes students continue to expect "professional homogeneity" after they arrive. Socializers, however, can deal with this discrepancy by challenging the notion that conventional kinds of homogeneity are necessary for community. They argue that your presence in the organization indicates that you should be there; that you are, or will become, the right kind of person. Faculty, then, redefine heterogeneity as positive, and they do this with some degree of success:

Most of my friends through college were people very similar to me, similar in background, height and weight, interests, average good looks. This is going to sound like a horrible thing to say, but I remember last year when I began to get to know Paula [a second-year student] that I had not been attracted to her immediately as someone to get to know—because of her weight problem, I'm sure. I remember talking with her one night, thinking, "This is one of the finest women I've ever known," thinking that I've never had a fat friend. This place has made me look at people deeper than what they look like on the outside. Here I'm exposed to people with a lot of different backgrounds, and there's something really neat about the fact that somehow we've all come to this place. . . . Somehow God was working [she said this laughing a little] or the spirit drew us here or something. That's neat and that provides a real bond between us that I never felt when I was in college. (Interview: female, second-year student)

According to socializers, diversity is a positive state that enriches community. For example, at the end of the first meeting of one advisory group, the professor said to her advisees, with enthusiasm: "We have such diversity here! It's marvelous! We each bring so much with us." Faculty say that differences among students and teachers are superficial and mask the real homogeneity that resides beneath. Socializers rationalize the discrepancy by differentiating "essences" from "exteriors" (see Hammersmith 1976), claiming that differences among recruits are superficial and exterior, but their commonalities are deep and essential. As an administrator said during his sermon, in an appeal to "essence": "We are all One at the Lord's table." We will see later that students also can use this technique to legitimate their violations of socializers' norms to themselves, to their peers, and to their socializing agents.

The legitimation of heterogeneity remains problematic, for students continue to discover differences in values that they define as relevant to community identification. Appealing to an inner essence does not specify which characteristics are superficialities and which are essential. Because socializers do not specify the dimensions of homogeneity, there seem to be endless possibilities for disappointments, including the discovery that a peer watches television five hours a day or participates in homosexual activities:

Most of the students had left the cafeteria [after dinner]. Carol and Susan and I were talking at one of the tables. Carol, a first-year Master of Christian Education student, said, "I was wondering if you've picked up on the lack of stability here." I said, "What do you mean?" She said, "Oh, I mean some of the people who are here. I mean, you wonder how they got through their boards!" [Church examining committees] Susan, a first-year ministry student, said, "Yeah, I know what you mean. Some of them, really!" I said, "Like who?" Susan said, whispering, "Well, look over to your right." Carol said, "Yes. Robert. He's one. Do you know he watches TV five hours a day? Can you believe that?" (Field notes)

*   *   *

I came here and found women into their own thing and men into theirs. [What do you mean?] Oh, women into their rights. . . . Another thing was smoking and drinking. These aren't *big* deals, but I was surprised to see so much of it. (Interview: male, first-year student)

Affect

Students expect their participation in a community to make them feel good. Faculty lead students to believe that these good feelings will come from being close to their peers and teachers. However, socializers do not regulate interpersonal relations between students outside of class, students do not all take the same classes, and teachers differ in the degree and kind of closeness they provide students. Consequently, students differ in how satisfied they feel with their seminary relationships, which in turn affects how likely they are to accept the demands faculty make in the name of the community.

Students who get to feel good come to value and appreciate

student life at the seminary and feel that the spirit of community is being realized. A few who had been reclusive as undergraduates but became popular in the seminary spoke with the most enthusiasm about community:

In junior high I was no one. I grew up with a lot of kids who would make good storm troopers. And I was target practice for 'em. At the same time, I was being exposed to the virtues of Christianity—humility, meekness, and mildness and all this—it kind of grew into a sickening kind of humility in which I would immediately defer to anyone. Well, things have been helpful since I came to seminary. The community I talk about has been very affirming, very supportive, and rather challenging as well. They say, "Why the hell don't you believe this about yourself, you're a good guy!" I've suddenly come to realize that that entails responsibility; that you are capable and people depend on you. Humility does not mean to deny what you're doing. (Interview: male, first-year student)

*   *   *

I found what I needed. I was accepted into the community. I was open for anything and I got everything. I was lucky to come in spring. The first quarter I was treated very specially because I was new, I could be friends with everybody. I got introduced around and got to know the whole campus right away. The next quarter, fall, I was still first-year officially, so I could get to know the first-year students, and if they had a question they came to me. . . . The messages that I had always given to people, "You're OK as you are, you don't have to be someone different, you don't need to be a father or spouse to be whole"—those messages didn't mean a thing if I didn't see myself as being whole. . . . I realized that I was whole, complete, and I got affirmation here in this community. (Interview: male, third-year student)

*   *   *

It's only since I've been at seminary that I've been able to recognize the need to have a community of people who you can dump everything in front of and who can be supportive and who can help. (Interview: male, second-year student)

Others, however, feel they do not get the kind or degree of affect they expect from community:

I guess I expected it [the seminary] to be motivated by some high standards of concern and caring. What I have in mind is an ideal, Christian community. I'm not saying I expected it to be *the* ideal, but it has fallen short in that regard. I've seen some things here that have indicated to me that people aren't as sensitive to the needs and cares of one another as they ought to be. And in a seminary community I expected it to be a little better than normal, and in some ways I found it to be worse. (Interview: female, third-year student)

Another student said bitterly:

Sure, they are *nice* to you, but they don't really care. (Field notes: male, first-year student)

Further, students change their acceptance or rejection of the community rhetoric over time, depending on ups and downs in their interpersonal relations at the seminary. For example, the following second-year student spoke of the common bond between students but also alluded to the problems of having her relationship with her fiancé become community property:

This place is different than other dorms. It's different in that we have a real common bond. Here we're studying the same thing, we're in the same classes, it's much more of a family type thing. . . . I miss being in an apartment, living in a dorm gets to be a fishbowl life. . . . I used to date a guy who's a second-year student. Last spring we were dating a lot. We had talked about getting married and all that . . .

A student threw an engagement party for himself [last spring] and people were coming up to John and me, because we had been dating seriously for about six weeks when Jeff got engaged. People were coming up to us and saying, "When are we going to hear from you two, ha ha ha," and that kind of thing. You don't need that kind of thing . . .

We broke up. And there's still real awkwardness being on campus with him. And he's got a new girlfriend on campus too. (Interview)

Not all students immediately define the organizational demand of self-disclosure as a positive emotional experience. Because most students are accustomed to choosing to whom they reveal private information, they must be convinced that the demands of self-disclosure are legitimate. Although the rhetoric of socializers is supposed to turn what students initially experience as a violation into a value, the process is not an automatic one, and students may define any particular demand as too demanding, as a negative affective experience that they find embarrassing or trying. Because faculty use "community" abstractly and ambiguously, students can define any particular demand as inappropriate to the rhetoric, or as a violation of community. Students, then, may turn the positive affect they associate with community, affirming, sharing, and caring from love to hate, from trust to distrust.

The organization, however, responds to this problem by bringing in other referents for "real" community and by making negative affect an important part of the rhetoric. Although "affirming" and other similar words suggest that students should feel good, socializers say that pain, as well as joy, is an important experience for becoming a community person and hence a good minister. Socializers subsume both positive and negative affect into a broader goal, growth. They argue that growth is facilitated by intense feelings, whether positive or negative. Schur (1976) noted this theme in the awareness movements of the 1970s, including the idea that pain must be risked in order to experience joy. The basic idea is that the routinization of feelings is bad, which implies that intense feelings of any kind are ultimately good. For example, during an orientation session, one of the administrators emphasized that the advisory groups (eight students who meet once a week with their adviser) are supposed to be support groups, but

are not a hand-holding society. They are a place to share joys and fears together. They are a place where you reflect on the nature of ministry in a small group and discuss your readiness for ministry. (Field notes: second day of orientation, Fall 1978)

In certain classes, faculty equated the value of suffering and hate with that of joy and love. Further, in some self-disclosure sessions, teachers told students to challenge each other and express their feelings, no matter what they were. Therefore, socializers who encourage negative affect partly take care of the discrepancy between the ideal of "feeling good" the rhetoric conveys and the reality. As one student wrote in the subsection of her ministry project called "Community":

Intimacy with others is something which requires oftentimes painful exposure and honesty, careful concern for others which is frequently draining and the ability to realize the meaning of commitment. Despite the effort demanded, however, there is no substitute for the continued affirmation and continued challenging found in a covenant community.

Students' disappointment in the kind of affect they received and challenges to it were not problems the organization could resolve once and for all (even within a given cohort or a given year). Because students learned to think about all events in terms of feelings, they could judge any act as worthy or not of community.

Violating the "Spirit of Community"

Some students felt that the existence of small groups calling themselves "communities" violated faculty's suggestion that the seminary constituted a community as a whole. Some of the groups are created by the organization, such as the fairly separate black program and women's program and the existence of the black caucus and the women's caucus. The faculty and administrators know that the students may find the existence of these groups a threat to a sense of community in the school, and they try to deal with it. For example, in his orientation speech, one of the administrators said, "We are all One in the Body of Christ, all one Community." Later in the speech he said:

Some students say there should be peace and sharing; that's not the reality. We need to know that blacks in our time have certain problems that others don't, and so do women.

The administrator, then, is saying at least implicitly that the existence of these groups does not contradict community. Students, however, respond with ambivalence to such statements:

I was at first disappointed to find that the black caucus was so separatist and whites were willing to [let that happen] and encouraging that to happen. I've been liberated or unliberated to the point that I can see reasons for the separation; well, not the reason, but the rationale. I'm still disappointed, but I'm not waving banners or anything. (Interview: male, second-year student)

*   *   *

Six of us [three males and three females] were talking in Jill's room. I asked Randy, one of the second-year students who was working at orientation, "Is the [orientation] program any diferent this year?" Randy said, "Pretty much the same. There is one difference, though. Last year when [the administrator] gave his speech about how, despite our diversity, we're really One? Well, last year the speech was the same, but right afterward he had someone from the black caucus talk about the black church and the black experience; then he had a woman talk about, rather, gripe about, women's concerns. At the end we thought, "If this is being a community of one, let's not know about our diveristy!" (Field notes)

The students are concerned with maintaining the spirit of community in the seminary (shown by their disappointment in the school's failure to always uphold it). But they also want to have more intimate relationships with a few people—small "communities"—which they know may work against the spirit of community in the school. They, like most people, want friends and romantic relationships. These small groups are especially important to them because they are the main arena in which they may engage in religious talk and prayer.

Students do have small groups of friends, but, knowing that the existence of these groups may contradict "community," they are sometimes quite secretive about them. Most learn not to display openly that they spend much of their time with a few close friends. Students frowned on friendship groups that violated that norm, calling them "cliques." Those who complained about cliques would refer to their own friendship group as an "affinity group," "support group," or a "community"—terms commensurate with a spirit of community.

One group whose members were quite open about its existence was sometimes gossiped about as cliquish:

At breakfast one of the second-year students asked me, "Have you noticed any cliques?" I said, "What do you mean?" Gail said, "Well, one first-year student was talking to me and she said there's this one clique here, and she just can't get to know the people in it. . . . This person hangs around with upper-year students, mainly because she can't seem to get to know these people. . . . When I lived in Billings [dorm] last year we didn't really have any cliques. Surely you got closer with some people more than with others, but there weren't larger groups people were excluded from. On the whole, we were together. (Field notes)

That secrecy is normative in creating small groups is evidenced in the following:

Within a month after I came here [in midyear] a guy who lived across the hall from me was a member of a . . . just a sharing group, a support group I guess one could call it. They were looking for three new persons. They wanted to keep their numbers small and intimate. And they'd been watching the new students for several months and they called on me and asked me if I'd be interested in that. And I said yeah, 'cause I feel the need for that kind of support. [What years were these students in?] A couple of the students were third-years, a couple were second-year and they were getting a few first-years. (Interview: male, second-year student)

Small groups were in fact taken very seriously, for this is where discussions deemed inappropriate in public could take place. Hence, students would self-consciously decide what they wanted to discuss in the group. For example, one group of students who made vegetarian dinners together at one of the married student's apartments every Saturday night had trouble deciding what kind of group they wanted to be. After we returned from one of the dinners, a member of the group talked to me about it:

Mindy feels that Saturday night should be a time to relax and that we have enough theologizing all week. You see, Margaret started this meeting on Saturday nights because she felt that she's out of the community by being married and living off campus, and she wanted to theologize with people. So it started off with Margaret, Mindy, and myself. Then, Beth and Hillery were invited, mainly 'cause Mindy and I got to know Beth. Hillery, as you've probably noticed, pretty much keeps to herself, so she stopped coming. Beth still comes, but sometimes she babysits, like tonight. Don and Patrick also got invited early on. At one point Beth wanted to turn this into a support group, a community. She wanted to be able to bring up anything that was bothering her to the group and we'd discuss it. [Where did she bring this up?] She told it to me, and to Mindy and to Margaret separately, then it became a group discussion one Saturday night. . . . It was also there that Mindy told us her feelings about the group, that it should be a fun group and not a theological one. (Field notes: female, first-year student)

Romantic couples felt they shouldn't openly spend much time together for fear of violating the spirit of community. Because many couples kept their relationship private, the students were often surprised when their friends suddenly announced their engagement:

Someone tells you they're going to get married. I used to think, how can you possibly be surprised? But I *have* been surprised. I have been surprised by at least half the couples I have known who have gotten married. I didn't even know they were going out. . . . A good friend of mine, in my first year here, who lived upstairs . . . suddenly said she was getting married. All of us in the dorm were fairly close and we were all surprised. (Interview: female, third-year student)

Ironically, students often felt a friend had violated a community norm by hiding the fact that he was dating someone seriously. They felt, How could I have been close to this person if she was involved with someone and I didn't even know about it? The friend, however, is caught in a double bind. To make the relationship public is to threaten the spirit of community and to have the relationship become community property; to disclose the information later is to risk losing one's friends. Students, then, found it difficult to develop romantic relationships in the context of community norms. For example, Marie, a second-year student, wanted to discuss future career plans with her seminary boyfriend:

I don't know if I can talk to him about it. Actually, the problem is *when* can I talk to him about it? There's always people in his room or my room. If I go down there, Bill or Eric or David will be there, watching the news. If I'm there alone with Sean, people will hear my voice and come over. You know, if someone's with him they think it's OK to visit. And you know about 10 P.M. cocoa, everyone [in the group] just comes here. (Field notes)

In addition to wanting close friendships and romantic relationships, students also want to exclude certain peers from their daily interactions simply because they don't like them. However, because of the espoused spirit of community students could not exclude others purposefully without feeling guilty. They learned to use the ambiguous rhetoric of community to legitimate the exclusion of others, just as the faculty and administrators used it to justify the existence of various communities within the school.

When students dislike a particular person and exclude him from their interactions, they claim that the person has not learned to act like a real community person and that the exclusion will teach him to do otherwise. During the research, there were three male students who most of the other students disliked (although the three knew each other, they did not constitute a group). Students often showed their dislike through the "nonperson" treatment, managing to ignore them, interrupt, or "talk over" them, or leave without saying good-bye to them. These tactics occurred often at mealtimes in the cafeteria, and in other public areas of the seminary. When I questioned a male, first-year student about how recruits treated one of the marginal students, he said:

It's best that we ignore him. That way he'll mellow out, he'll learn he can't dominate. It's best for *him* . . . I think he *is* mellowing out a little. (Field notes)

Students do sometimes recognize contradictions between their behavior and their espoused ideals and use the seminary rhetoric to come to terms with their dislike. For example, in a dorm suite, two second-year students (one male and one female) were gossiping about two of the disliked students. The male student suddenly said:

This is terrible. Let's not talk about them anymore. They're part of this community. I think we have to love them as much as we can. (Field notes)

White students use the rhetoric to justify the fact that white students and black students, by and large, segregate themselves. Students are reminded of this at mealtimes in the cafeteria, when the black students sit together at a separate table, at a distance from the white students. Some white students say that this segregation contradicts community and, since they share the view that they (not the black students) are responsible for making the first move, they feel guilty. My notes indicate that the white students make few moves, but that they use the community rhetoric to justify their nonaction and the continuation of segregation. They argue that community is reached through diversity, does not require interaction, and therefore can be realized with black students they have little to do with. Participants in the Women's Theologizing Group made this view explicit:

Phyllis, a second-year student, said, "I think there's community here in this room tonight. It's not what I expected community to be when I got here [to the seminary], but I don't think it's superficial, either . . ." A third-year woman said, "Last year in [theology] class there was this couple who always complained about the lack of community. It made me sick after a while. . . . They think community is patting each other on the back and bluebirds singing." The others laughed. Phyllis said, "Yes, I think we find community through diversity. When I don't accept community, it's when I don't accept diversity. Like I feel community with the blacks even though they have their own caucus and sit at their own table. I don't actually have to commune with them to experience community with them." The others nodded. (Field notes: meeting room, five women present)

These students use the same tactic that faculty use to deal with the discrepancy between students' expectation of homogeneity and the existence of heterogeneity. Both groups appeal to "essence," to the idea that they are all "One," despite any difference in attribute or action or lack of interaction.

Disliked students, however, can also use community norms to get some of the spirit of community from their peers. For example, near the close of some worship services in the seminary, the program calls for "passing the peace." During this ritual, people usually give a gesture of affection (most often, hugs) to the persons sitting close by. If one stands at the back of the chapel it appears that everyone is hugging and that community is being realized. However, friends tend to sit with friends (or at least people they like somewhat), and the hugging is patterned. Because the community rhetoric provides a definition of the situation which specifies that "everyone loves everyone," the disliked students can take advantage of this definition and hug the people around them, even when their peers seem uncomfortable during the act. In this situation, everyone knows that to push the disliked student away or tell him to stop is to commit a heresy. Therefore, students can use the rhetoric to control and be controlled by their peers.

Community as a Cliché

Students become upset when they discover that their teachers or peers have discrepant meanings for words they care about. For example, note the reactions of two students who discover their apparent agreement about community is only an appearance:

I was in Marsha and Barbara's room. Bill, Barbara's fiancé, was also there. [All three are first-year students.] Marsha said, "It was strange in class today. People were talking about their placements for next year. She then listed the churches where the graduating students would be working as ministers next year. "Also, Sylvia's going on intern next year and Wendy is moving out of the dorm [into married student housing]." Barbara nodded and said, "Yes, it's going to be strange. I don't think I'll get together with the new students next year." Marsha looked upset and said, "Barbara, how can you say that?" Barbara replied, "Well, when I think of the community I think of Wendy and Sylvia and you and most of the people in the dorm. With a lot of them gone, the community's gone." Marsha said, "I don't see how you can say that, that that's community. Just think if the second-year people had thought that when *we* first arrived, we wouldn't have gotten to know them." (Field notes)

Socializers and recruits use community and other words so often and in so many ways that recruits sometimes think others use the words merely as clichés. As one student remarked about the word "theologize":

Every time we turned around, the school or classes or somebody was telling us to theologize about our experience. It's still a joke now. [So, it became a joke?] Yes, it got tiring. Most of it came from colloquium, you've probably heard about that. Every time we'd go out and do something we'd have to come back and theologize about that experience. So we made jokes about theologizing about going to the bathroom, you know, the idea that everything can be theologized about. (Interview: female, third-year student)

Once students think others mean nothing when they use the words, they are also likely to think others' usages indicate a pretense of commitment. They think others use the words insincerely and as a means to control them. That students sometimes think their socializers use the words in shallow ways is hinted at in the following exchange:

About six males were eating dinner at one table when I walked into the cafeteria. Greg [a first-year student] jumped up and said, "Let's get another table to attach to this one so Sherryl can eat with us." I proceeded to buy my meal and sat down at the table Greg and Earl had moved for me. Then, three female students [two first-year, one second-year] came into the room. Greg again jumped up and moved another table to the end of mine. He said, laughing, "See? We'll have community!" Everyone chuckled. (Field notes)

Greg suggests here that members of the organization at least sometimes have simplistic notions about community, believing that building one is as easy as moving a few tables together.

Students learn to anticipate others' challenges to their commitment to the spirit of community:

Tonight one second-year woman and three first-year women and I went out for ice cream. Driving back in her car, the second-year woman said, "Is anyone going to the [spring] dance?" One of the first-year women said, "No, I don't know how to dance, really. Professor James asked us if we'd like to get out of class early to go to the dance, but no one said yes." Another first-year woman said, "I might go. You gonna go, Sherryl?" I said, "I might. I like to dance." The second-year woman sighed and said, "I can see it now. Not many women will go and the men will say it's because the women have problems relating to men, and that we should all be together, a nice community, all One in the Body of Christ." (Field notes)

They also learn to respond to those challenges:

I was visiting Celia, a third-year student, at her apartment in the city (about a half hour's drive from the seminary) with Kate, a first-year student. Celia said, "Today Beverlee [third-year student] and Brian [third-year student] were trying to talk me into taking an apartment that opened up [in married student housing]." She sounded a little angry. I said, "So?" Celia said, "Well, this is probably the last time I'll get to live in a big city, I know I'll be in rural areas for a long time. But Beverlee and Brian were saying, 'This is the last year you can live in the community; you should be at the seminary.' And I kept thinking, 'There's something wrong with that logic,' but I couldn't think of what. Then, finally, it hit me. I have other communities too, like the one here, the people at the church I worked at last year. And it comes down to, I don't want to be with the people there [at the seminary] all the time. And I hate the way they make it sound like if I don't go back there to live that I'm rejecting them. It means that I don't want to be around them all the time, but it doesn't mean that I'm rejecting them." (Field notes)

Once students think faculty or friends are pretending to care, they may question the trust that is the basis for disclosing personal information. Since it is personnel who convince recruits to trust each other and them through the community rhetoric, students may question organizational demands when they find out that others share the words, but not the meaning. Some simply stop telling other students and faculty as much as they used to. The following student was very bitter about it:

Close friends are hard to get anywhere. . . . Here it's very hard because you tell one person something and they feel they're doing you a favor by telling their closest friend, and so on. [He proceeded to give me lengthy examples.] Students feel that because this is a community setting everyone *should be* sharing things. Last year there was this big thing about journals, everyone pouring their hearts out. For the first week I did what everyone else was doing, writing very personal things. I also was feeling that I was losing a lot of integrity—I didn't really know the faculty members reading it. I decided I just wasn't going to hand it in. (Interview: male, second-year student)

Most students do not go this far. (I know of only one other student, a first-year woman, who refused to hand in her journal, an assignment for the only required course in the first year of study.) My notes show that a number of students said to me and to others that the student in the above quotation was "too rational" and not "open enough," suggesting that while most become cynical about the humanistic rhetoric at times, they do not offer much resistance. Once recruits think faculty use a word illegitimately to get them to do things, it also becomes possible for students to use the ambiguous rhetoric to challenge the faculty. For example:

In class, the professor spoke of the seminary as a community. A male, second-year student, said, "Well, I don't know. I have friends that I've just about given up on. They rarely call on me; I'm always calling on them. And you say we're supposed to be part of this Christian community?" (Field notes)

Here, the student is challenging socializers' ideal picture of the world as well as his peers' behavior. When there was a threat that two students would be dismissed for homosexual activities, recruits opposing the action used the rhetoric of community to make their case. In a meeting of fifty students and five faculty members, one male second-year student argued:

How can you call this a Christian community when you make people leave because of their sexual preference? (Field notes)

The four students who expressed the most cynicism and the most resistance to the demands of socializers were also the least cynical about the ideals represented by the rhetoric. Why? These students felt that socializers sometimes used the rhetoric in manipulative ways, but they did not relinquish the ideals along with the rhetoric. In fact, they were angry that others discredited the ideals by abusing words like "community" and "affirming." While any student can question the words and demands of the faculty, those who care the *most* are most likely to resent others who show a pretense of commitment. Similarly, Keniston (1968) found that student radicals strongly held the principles, but not the practices, of their parents, finding the latter discrepant with the former (see also Lipset and Albach 1968). Bennett (1965) found that architecture students whose ideals matched those of the faculty were most likely to drop out of the program. And, Olesen and Whitaker (1968, 135) found that drop-outs at a nursing school had scored higher on faculty ideals ("nonauthoritarianism," "complexity," "impulse expression") than students who made it through the program.

In a quite different context and from the perspective of an economist, Hirschman (1970) has argued that people who value the quality of a product or organization more than the price will be the first to leave if the quality declines, regardless of price. Further, he argued that those who stay when the quality declines may be the ones to exhibit "voice," that is, who fight for raising the quality.

If one conceives of a making-the-grade perspective as "price" and the community perspective as "quality," it makes sense, using Hirschman's argument, that those who are most disappointed by discrepancies between the ideals and reality also exhibited voice. I found that the disillusioned students alternated between voicing their dissatisfaction and withdrawing. What seems to happen is the following. These students stay in the organization and speak up because they care about the ideals and want to fight for them. The more they fight, the more they recognize discrepancies between the ideals and reality. Consequently, at times they just don't think the organization deserves their idealism. They then withdraw from others, from the community. They can justify being reclusive to themselves, in part, by saying the place doesn't deserve their idealism. Because they are idealists, however, they cannot justify staying in the organization just to get the degree but must think the community has intrinsic value. Hence, during the stages of withdrawal, they come to focus on the organization's good points. But by believing, once again, that the organization does resemble a "community" in some ways, that it is salvageable, they find themselves turning their disillusionment once again into "voice." For example, a second-year male student who alternated between periods of withdrawal and periods of complaining about his peers' and teachers' lack of caring had this to say in an interview when I asked him about his search for community at the seminary:

Yeah, community in the sense that a group of people with related ideas, understandings, common goals; I was expecting a modern utopia here [laughing] in the sense that you could get to know people on a more sincere basis, not because you feel obligated to get to know them, but because you want to. . . . I think it's a matter of getting used to the idea that seminary is not that much different from any other school. A lot of people enter the seminary thinking that they're going to be able to make friends much easier, much closer friendships, that the administration's going to be far more open to students, teachers will be friendlier, and it just doesn't happen. . . . You have as much backstabbing and politics here. . . .

You *do* have the positive points, too, they're not as obvious as you anticipated them to be. . . . There is more concern here for other people. But, at times that concern can become overwhelming in that it becomes only a probing into your private life. This has to be done *carefully*; that's what I want.

Another of the disillusioned, Kristin, exhibited the most voice about women's and gay rights in the seminary. I met her in her third year, when she alternated between fighting and withdrawing.

I thought perhaps there would be more community and more caring for other people . . . because of the supposed Christian commitment. And I find people run up against that a lot here. They think, "Here we are in a supposed loving, caring, Christian community," and yet people are being shat upon and destroyed by either policy or people's attitudes because they're different . . . It [affirming] is ambiguous. I think people use the word "affirm" because it *is* so ambiguous. I can say "I affirm you," which doesn't call for any real commitment. You know, affirming in the "I'm OK—You're OK" approach. Then, there's affirming that means "I think that what you are and what you stand for are excellent and I will work on it with you and fight for it." And it becomes a crime not to affirm people. And I get in trouble sometimes because I say that some people on this campus should not be affirmed, they should be challenged. You can say, "Yes, you're a good, worthy, treasure-of-God person, but what you feel and what you are, are lousy." I do not affirm you, then . . .

I think that more one-to-one relationships develop [in seminary] when someone sees that someone is hurting, it's the pastoral in people. [What kinds of hurting?] Oh, depression, or say, if someone's mother or father dies. People will talk about what to do and who should talk to the person. And it's not catty talk, it's genuine. Even mood changes. Like if I withdraw for a while, people in the hall whom I've hardly talked to at all will come round and say "Are you alright?" Which is nice—sometimes; other times you wish they'd just let you withdraw. It's really noticeable how that happens. (Interview)

Despite her disillusionment, Kristin and two other idealists opted to stay in the dorm for first-year people in order to integrate the new women into the community. The two other women also suggested to the administration that some upper-year women attend orientation in order to meet the new students.

IMPLICATIONS

When students begin their professional studies, they often assume that the collectivity they will eventually enter is distinctive and esteemed. Such a conception of the professional body presumes that the profession is homogeneous rather than comprising segments which may compete or conflict with each other. They may learn, for example, that the profession includes specialties or subfields. Consequently, they may come to identify with a subgroup. It is likely, however, that they will still identify with the larger professional title, for the title confers the idea that the occupation is distinct from other professions and more esteemed than many occupations.

Midwest Seminary is probably similar to other professional programs in suggesting that the profession is a community, a whole. Ironically, social control of students becomes problematic partly because the faculty and administrators make too much of unity within the field. By using the term "community" so often, they overemphasize the idea that the profession is made up of like-minded individuals. This makes students sensitive to discrepancies between the ideal of similarity and sympathy and the reality of diversity. At the same time, socializers make individual differences the basis of professional distinctiveness. The faculty suggest the following paradox: Professional authority is anchored in the individual rather than in the institution, yet there is a basic homogeneity that makes ministers a professional community. This contradiction makes it difficult for students to assume that the professional body exists and knows best. Since community is the rhetoric the faculty use to establish students' trust in them, students raise questions about the legitimacy of the program's demands.

Other professional programs, by making the symbols of professional power unambiguous, probably treat professional homogeneity and specialness as assumptions rather than constantly talk about them. In addition, socializers probably downplay individual differences, conceiving of them as personal styles ("bedside manner") which merely color the institutional authority of the professional. In such a situation, students are more likely to assume that the professionals know best and to get on with their work.

6

Female Students' Dilemmas

In the context of Midwest Seminary, "humanism" is a prescriptive term; it suggests ways of acting and thinking that all human beings should endorse. Faculty imply that treating people in a personal and egalitarian fashion is simply a good human orientation. Traditionally, however, it is women who have held the nurturant role in societies and have tended to personalize human relations. This does not mean that men do not care about interpersonal relations nor that women cannot engage in instrumental tasks. What it does mean is that women have more often than men been given the task of caring for others and hence dealing with personalized relations. In addition, since women do not, by and large, have the authority generally vested in males (regardless of their other statuses), they have been less likely to act authoritatively with others. Women have tended toward more personalized and egalitarian relations with others than have men (Boulding 1977). It is fitting, then, that Douglas (1977) calls Protestant ministers' ideological response to deprofessionalization a "feminizing" of their former beliefs.

The ministry is a traditional, male-dominated profession, one that has allowed women access only recently. Women who enter male-dominated settings are likely to have several problems. As

Kanter convincingly argued in her 1977 study of men and women of the corporation, women face the problems of tokenism when they are a numerical minority. Related to the problems women face in going to a male-dominated professional school, they may also face the problems of being in a male-oriented setting. Besides being a numerical minority, they may, depending on the profession, also be a cultural minority.

The traditional role of the minister fits with the stereotypical male model of behavior. Since ministers are supposed to be authoritative and somewhat authoritarian, personable but not personal, we would expect women entering the field to feel somewhat uncomfortable. Midwest Seminary, however, is humanistically oriented. Thus, the women who go there should have their time made easier because of the prevailing "feminized" ideology. Humanism, by espousing personal and egalitarian relations with others, is firmly set against the traditional male model of ministerial behavior. Assuming that the female students at Midwest Seminary have had some prior socialization toward the nurturing role, they should feel more comfortable with humanistic ideas and behaviors than with traditionalism.[1]

Midwest Seminary in fact encourages women to apply to the seminary, offers a special program for women, and has a student women's caucus. The program should provide the female students with an ideal setting to do the traditional "male task" of achieving in a profession, especially one that is male-dominated. Since people generally see "woman" and "minister" as contradictory statuses, the program's emphasis on women should help the female students see their two roles as complementary. The women students are entering a school with a feminized ideology and support groups that should help them with the particular problems they face as women in a professional school. The seminary, then, provides an interesting case to see what happens to women who are studying in a male-dominated but female-oriented school that has set up special programs to help them. Given an ideology that sug-

---

1. Recent work on children's moral development (Gilligan 1982) and children's games (Lever 1976) indicates that girls are more concerned than boys with relationships and are more sensitive to the needs of others.

gests "all are called to minister," we might expect them to have an easier time becoming committed to the ministry as a career than women in other male-oriented professional schools.

However, since the women students expect parishioners not only to challenge their nontraditional professional ideology but their claim to the ministerial role as well, they feel an even greater need than the men to have a firm sense of professional authority in their future relations with clients. The women students at Midwest Seminary are placed in a situation where they cannot fully accept the rhetoric and ideology lest they diminish the role-model strength needed to survive in a male-dominated field.

CONTRADICTIONS OF STATUS

Almost all of the Midwest Seminary students have trouble thinking of themselves as the kind of people who will become ministers. Initially, they think of ministers as superior figures they are not worthy of being or they have some friends who frown upon religion. Although the students learn to demystify the image of the minister, they expect parishioners to treat them in traditional ways. The women, however, have an additional problem: they know that being a woman and a minister is a contradiction both for those who ridicule religion and those who revere it (Charlton 1978).

Most of the women had to deal with this contradiction before they came to seminary. One way they talked about this problem was by complaining that they had not had a role model. The men I interviewed and talked with never mentioned this problem. This is not to suggest that most of the men had a specific minister who encouraged them to go to seminary, although some did. But the male students had at least seen, since childhood, men who were ministers. Many of the women, on the other hand, had never seen, let alone known, a female minister. They not only lacked encouragement from a particular female minister but lacked a general role model as well. Even a student whose father was a minister and, by her account, encouraged her and her sisters to "achieve" talked about the problem of not having had a role model:

Going into ministry was never something I had been told *not* to do, but I also didn't have very many people to turn to who were in that role. That's where this school in particular seemed to be so appropriate, because they were saying, "Hey, women, it's OK, we want you here." (Interview: first-year student)

That others regard the female and ministerial roles as contradictory is also shown by the reactions the women received from their parents, relatives, friends, and hometown parishioners. For example, two women reported that others said they should become ministers' wives rather than ministers when they announced their occupational plans:

My father is really old-fashioned. The idea of women in the ministry is still a little bit too much for him. I talked to him about my decision this summer and he said, "You know, I can imagine you with a husband and family. You'd made a good minister's wife. I mean, frosting on the cake—you can even play the piano." He couldn't see me as a minister. (Interview: second-year student)

Relatives, friends, and others varied in their responses to the women's announcements. Some women claimed they were raked up and down the coals for doing something "unnatural for women." Others found acceptance of their decisions from friends who treated the recruit as if she were suddenly an authoritative figure. Hence, the image of the minister is sometimes strong enough to override the conventional contradiction between being a woman and a minister. Most of the women, however, had to deal with negative reactions from one or more audiences, and generally they are aware that others, whether now or when they practice ministry, will challenge their right to be ministers:

Some people say that women just shouldn't be ministers, and use examples from the Bible. So I guess it's worse than when some people think that women shouldn't be doctors, say, or some other male type of profession. These are warped examples, in my opinion, but they're used. Like one typical example is Paul, the apostle, writes that women should not speak in the church service and their place is beneath the man's. He writes that the man is the head of the Church. But the problem with the example is that they're taking it out of historical context. Paul was saying that women could participate in the service to a certain degree, at least, which was *radical* at the time. But people don't see that. They just pull the sentence out of the text. 'Cause Paul said at another point that in Christ there is no male or female. That doesn't mean you're supposed to deny your sexuality or anything, but that everyone is equal. (Field notes: female, first-year student)

One common discrimination against women in the professions is the feeling that "woman" and "professional" just do not go together. Related to this denial of status is the conventional notion that women, because of competing family obligations, cannot be as committed to their careers as men. A more subtle part of the discriminatory environment for female professional students is the fact that work organization and careers are based on conventional notions of the male role in the family and the male biological "clock" (Bourne and Wikler 1978). Women are usually expected to marry and have children (and to be the main caregivers) at an age when men are expected to settle into a career. Even if others do not question their future commitment, women have learned that having both a family and career may be difficult. The female students worried about these future problems and we will see how the ideology played a part in how they handled them.

In sum, people outside the organization and conventional notions drawn from prior socialization experiences made the women aware of the difficulties they might encounter as female ministers. Further, the women were aware that not all churches accept them; most seminaries are less receptive to women than Midwest Seminary, and some district committees are uneasy about accepting women into the ministry at all.

INSIDE THE ORGANIZATION

Outside expectations alone make the women students aware of contradictions between their statuses as women and ministers. They know they will have to deal with these problems when they graduate and become ministers. In the meantime, does the seminary offer them an ideology which will mitigate the problem of this contradiction?

Inside the seminary, the existence of "women's courses" and the women students' caucus seems to have a boomerang effect. The emphasis on women made the female students acutely aware of how anomalous their position is; they acquired a heightened sense of the problem of their contradictory statuses. The students spent most of their time at women's caucus meetings talking about the problem of legitimating themselves as ministers. They talked about whether they should become political activists about the place of women in the ministry or a support group for each other (both concerns suggest they have problems men do not have). One concern often talked about was the presence of sexist language and ideas in theological writings, classes, and hymns, such as the reference to God the Father. They discussed whether the seminary should state as its policy that only inclusive (nonsexist) language be used by people giving talks at the seminary. Students differed in how radical they were about these issues; some felt they should not decide who should and should not talk, since humanism suggests they are open to all views. The toleration implied in humanism made it difficult for the women to take a stand against others' use of sexist language. Most of the women, however, felt that "inclusive language" was important and good. Since it is the humanistic ideology ("all are called") which legitimates their position as women ministers, to reject humanism would have made it difficult for them to accept their own place within the ministry. Their concern with inclusive language is, then, a concern about their legitimacy—to argue for inclusive language is to argue for an equal place in the ministry.

Hence, although some of the men thought the sheer existence of an all-female group indicated that the women were antimale, most of the issues discussed at women's caucus meetings centered on getting women included, rather than on excluding men. For example, the women used the term "inclusive" language rather than "nonsexist," "degendered," or some other term. The women rarely talked against men but about how they could legitimate themselves in a male-dominated profession and especially to traditional clients. In fact, they discussed how to legitimate themselves to female as much as to male parishioners.

The women's caucus, then, made women *more* aware of their minority position in the ministry and how parishioners might react to them. In fact, some women who had received few challenges to their occupational plans before coming to seminary learned to anticipate negative reactions from outsiders.

REACTIONS TO HUMANISM

Does humanism help resolve the contradiction? The women and men were ambivalent about the humanistic messages. Some of the women's ambivalence is related to their problem of trying to use the humanistic ideology to legitimate themselves to outsiders. We can see this by examining their reactions to courses on women.

Elsewhere I indicated that the women liked one of the three female faculty members the best because they thought her "the most human" and very interested in people. They liked one other woman (who held a mix of humanistic and traditional views) but felt the third female faculty member was too intellectual, too unconcerned with interpersonal relations, and "acted like a man." These data indicate that the students accepted the feminizing of the humanistic rhetoric.

The picture, however, is more complicated. Students' general ambivalence is also found more specifically in the female students' reactions to a women's course that they disliked immensely. This course was taught by a married couple who were visiting the seminary for a quarter. The course, which I attended three times, certainly emphasized humanism but did not strike me as being qualitatively different from other such courses (including courses for men and women). The women, it seemed to me, overreacted to the course—they felt it was "shallow" and "manipulative." These adjectives have been used by some authors to describe awareness movements generally. But given the students' general acceptance of experiential learning, it did not make sense that the women would react so negatively to this particular course. They complained angrily about the course at length over several lunches and organized their resistance; six of them talked to the couple after class and asked them to change the course. This is another indicator of the strength of their reaction; usually when students thought a course was too intellectual, they looked bored in class and complained only among themselves.

At lunch, six of the women were complaining about the Worship from a Feminist Perspective course. Bonnie said, "I can't take that class, I'm thinking of dropping out. Do you know what they made us do? They said to think of a food you want to give someone and give it to that person. I was sick! I just wouldn't do it. So the guy who teaches the course came over and said 'I'd like to give you mixed fruit.' I wanted to say 'I'd like to give you a punch in the mouth. . . .'" Carol said, "Then there was the time we were supposed to reflect on someone and see the light emanating from them, at Epiphany, which symbolizes light. God! The best was when they passed around a nail, and we were supposed to feel the nail going through our hand, to feel the pain Christ felt at the crucifixion. Ugh." (Field notes)

Not only did the women accept similar behavior in other classes I attended, but when I questioned them about what was so bad about the class they could not explain it. When I pointed out that similar activities occurred in other classes, they seemed exasperated, as if it were perfectly clear that the activity was acceptable in one context but not in the other. For example, one of the women complained that the couple started each class with a prayer, and that prayer was not appropriate for the classroom, "it just doesn't work." When I mentioned, however, that another class she was taking started with a prayer, she said it was acceptable there because it was "different." The difference, it seems, lies in the different criteria the women used to evaluate women's courses and general courses. The students felt a women's course should be experiential but should also provide intellectual and theological justification for women's participation in the ministry and feminist or innovative worship. Consider the following interchange:

Mary said, "I really thought the course was going to be good—worship from a feminist perspective sounded intriguing. I thought it would be more academic." Judy said, "Yes, we need more of a theological base for what we're doing. That's what we need from a course like this." Some of the women talked about how they had complained to the couple teaching the course. I said, "How did they react? What did they say?" Bonnie said, "They said they would try to change. Next week we're going to talk about inclusive language and the theological basis for it. That should be good." (Field notes)

The women, while accepting a feminized ideology and way of approaching the ministry that is fairly expressive and experiential, anticipate that they will have to legitimate themselves to others and hence want some intellectual justification for their future role. They largely endorse humanism, for that ideology legitimates their position in the profession; it is also a perspective they value.

They have some sense, however, that parishioners will define an extreme humanistic orientation not only as nontraditional (and hence illegitimate) but also as *feminine*. Since the minister's authority rests partly in the male status, the women will have a hard time proving that they are as good as male ministers if the male role is feminized. To act mainly in personal and egalitarian ways is to act "feminine" and hence to indicate further to parishioners that they are not "real" ministers (i.e., authority figures). Other indicators of the women's ambivalence to the humanistic role is shown by the following comment of a first-year woman:

Wasn't that interesting in class today, talking about how women always qualify their statements. They say 'maybe' or 'I think this is the case,' or 'if you want to do this, it's all right.' I'm really going to learn to undo that. When you're a minister the congregation expects you to know what you're doing, so you'd better take responsibility for it. None of this 'maybe' stuff. (Field notes)

ANTICIPATING A FAMILY AND CAREER

The humanistic ideology and role do not necessarily help the women resolve the problem of their contradictory statuses. It suggests acting in ways that are "feminine" and hence would not help others see them as authoritative professionals. Does the ideology help them to cope with the more subtle effects of discrimination that force them to juggle career and family in ways that men generally do not?

Some of the women note that district committees sometimes ask them pressing questions about their future marriage and family plans. For example, one of the women spoke about her experience with the district committee before the women's caucus meeting started:

Marcie was joking sarcastically about the meeting she had had with her district committee. She said, "They didn't ask me about my theology, just my sex life. They must have bothered me for about fifteen minutes, though I could have covered it in five." The women sitting by her laughed. Elaine said, "There's still hope. They asked me about my theology." Marcie continued, "They also bugged me about getting married. One man kept badgering me and when he finally said, 'Do you want to get married?' I said, 'Is that a proposal?'" The women laughed. (Field notes)

Although Marcie implicitly suggests that this district committee did not take her as seriously as a man in that the members cared more about her marriage plans than her theology, she, and most of the other female students, did not recognize what else the committee members' questions might have meant. It is possible that they were trying to find out if the woman will be committed to the ministry. As Bourne and Wikler (1978) pointed out in their study of a medical school, faculty often ask women about their marriage plans to test their future commitment to the profession. The faculty often assume that women who will marry and have children will be bad investments, will not work for long. Because the women students learn that the district committees also ask these questions of men, they do not think about the question as being unfair to women. The students discover that being married is an important auxiliary status for the minister, regardless of gender. Knowing this, the female students think that the district committees and others give men and women *equally* unfair treatment when asking about their future marriage and family plans. Even women who recognized that people do not think women ministers are likely to be as committed to their profession as men because of competing family obligations thought questions about marriage meant the same thing when asked of men:

I'm sure that if I were a guy people would have thought of it as a more serious commitment, but as a woman, people thought "You'll find a husband, maybe you'll be a minister, but you'll still get married." And I guess that's not just a female problem. In a class this morning one guy said he was told when he was in college heading towards seminary to get a wife and "it'll be easier to step into things." It's the minister, wife, and children role that everyone sees as the stereotype. (Interview: female, first-year student)

* * *

There isn't any rule written down, but the "married-minister-children" thing is important to get anywhere. So, for women it's doubly hard. First, you've got to find a church that will accept women; then, you've got to get married. (Interview: female, first-year student)

Although the district committees may not be testing the women's commitment, it is important that the women did not even suspect such a challenge to their professionalism.

Does this occur because the women do not see the possible

conflict of work and family obligations they may face in the future? Despite the women's interpretation of the district committee's questions, they do indeed expect to have trouble juggling a full-time career and a family. As the quote above suggests, the student recognized that people would have found her commitment to the ministry greater had she been a man, indicating the assumption that women will have competing family obligations. The women, however, accept the conventional assumption that it is the woman's responsibility to juggle career and home life (or to choose one or the other). They seem to accept the fact that they will have to deal with this situation but the male students will not. Much like Maines and Hardesty found in their study of undergraduate mathematics majors (1982), the women, but not the men, were concerned about how they would interweave future work and family roles. Similarly, Hammond found that only female medical students build "biographies as women who will postpone marrying and having children until after training, and yet who will not waste their training" (1980, 47).

The egalitarian rhetoric legitimates the women's right to have the same kind of professional commitment to the ministry as male ministers generally do. The women do not, however, recognize the contradiction between having an ideology which lets them in the profession and having to work that commitment around family plans while men do not. Instead of using the rhetoric to recognize and underline the inequality inherent in the situations facing professional men and women, they use it to accommodate their inequitable situation. What I found was that the women actually used the rhetoric to question their own commitment to the ministry. Since the humanistic ideology suggests that one can minister in all ways, some of the women, when considering the possible conflict between their family and career plans, talked about how they might really be called to be mothers and wives. Consider the following quote from a first-year woman who was dating a student at the seminary:

I don't know if I've been called to be ordained . . . [What's the hesitation?] I don't know. [What kind of difference does ordination make?] Well, one thing is they can send you anywhere they want. Well, if I thought I were called for sure I guess that wouldn't matter, right? [What are the alternatives to ordination?] I'm not sure, I haven't checked them out. But you can work for an organization affiliated with the Church without being sent around by the Church. [You keep mentioning this "being sent around"] OK, I have to admit I wouldn't be thinking about this as much if it weren't for Phillip. It has hit me that being an ordained minister could interfere with a family life. I've been brought up to think that it's the woman who should be flexible, that I'd go where the man would go. Before Phillip it was easy to think of being sent anywhere, but now it's different. It might not be Phillip I'll marry, but whoever it is, it could cause problems. I mean, maybe my calling is to be a housewife and mother? I don't know. (Interview)

Other women noted that once they are ministers, men might not be attracted to them, suggesting that people who do accept the woman as a minister cannot also accept that minister as a woman:

I feel I have a call to the ministry, it's not just something I'm doing because it's a nice job. I very much feel that call as a present reality, but I don't have a very strong sense of whether that is going to stay with me. I've got a lot of things I'm interested in, a lot of things I can do. I feel called to be a minister, now, at this time and in this place. And as long as I feel that call I'll remain a minister. When I feel that my call is to minister in some other way I may give it up and do something else. . . . I could have done ministry by remaining in the advertising business. . . . If I remain single and remain in the ministry, what about my private life? What if I go out and my date brings me back at three in the morning and the neighbors see that? And I also think, "Who in the world is going to want to take the minister out?" And, "Who am I ever going to meet?" The people I'm most likely to meet are people in my congregation. (Interview: female, second-year student)

The women, then, could provide a rationale for exiting from the seminary. If all callings are equal, then one can legitimately do something else instead, such as be a wife and mother. True, the men, too, could use this ideology to alleviate their sense of guilt or failure at leaving. Some men did say they might be called to do something else. This "something else," however, was always another profession. The men never talked about leaving because of being called to be husbands and fathers, but because they questioned their commitment to the ministry. The women who considered leaving tended not to allude to other professional callings, indicating that they were not rejecting ministerial work per se. In fact, the two women just quoted were the most active members of the seminary, were doing well in the program, were highly regarded by their classmates and teachers as people who would make good ministers, and talked enthusiastically about their work. It seems that once these women recognized how involved they were getting in their work they also realized that such a commitment could interfere with another important aspect of their lives in the future.

ANTICIPATING FUTURES

The humanistic ideology, role, knowledge, and rhetoric are not only incongruous with clients' future expectations, but also provide students with only a shaky basis of professional authority. Consequently, most of the students expect to have problems legitimating themselves as humanistic ministers to their parishioners. The problems the women anticipate, however, are different from the men's; the women also expect to legitimate their encumbency in the ministerial role.

The female students' concern about humanism can be understood in the light of the future problems they anticipate. On the one hand, the notion that all are called to minister legitimates their right to be ministers. On the other hand, fully accepting the humanistic role is tantamount to accepting conventionally feminine, and hence conventionally less authoritative, behavior. If the women fully adopt humanistic behavior, they will be giving up the few resources women in traditionally masculine positions of authority often use to legitimate themselves to clients.

Part of the authority of the minister's (and the professional's) role is rooted in the male status. It is understandable, then, that some women who enter male-oriented, as well as male-dominated professions, try to legitimate themselves, especially to clients, by acting "like men." In fact, some commentators have criticized the women's movement for failing to humanize relations, arguing that women who take on traditional male roles have "become men." It is important to recognize that in entering the professions as marginal members, malelike behavior is the resource available to women who seek recognition as professionals. In their attempts to be treated equally to men, some women have even disidentified from women generally (Heilbrun 1979), producing what has been called the Queen Bee syndrome.

In a male-dominated but female-oriented profession or professional school, one might expect women to refrain from emulating male behavior. I did find at Midwest Seminary that the women do not "act like men"; if anything, the men act somewhat "like women." Generally, both male and female students are expressive and engage in much emotion-talk. But in anticipation of their futures in a more traditional parish, the women remain ambivalent about the humanistic role. This suggests that the problems the male and female students face are qualitatively different. It is not simply that the men have one problem (legitimating the humanistic messages to parishioners) and the women have two (justifying their encumbency of the ministerial position as well as their humanism). The men rightly anticipate having fewer problems legitimating the humanistic role to parishioners because they are men. If Sennett is correct in asserting that people personalize work relations, clients may well view the male who acts humanistically as having the most acceptable professional style—he is not only competent, but "human" and "caring" as well. Parishioners may regard women who use the humanistic language, on the other hand, as simply "acting like women" and hence not acting like authority figures. Without having a convincing rhetoric of professional authority, the women cannot achieve the authority generally ascribed to male ministers. The women's anticipations may be realistic; they feel they cannot prove they are as competent as male ministers if they must appeal to an ideology which undermines authority generally and which calls for acting and thinking in ways conventionally associated with femininity. Others may regard the feminized male as human, and the feminized female as nonauthoritative. This suggests that despite the "feminization" of American culture, people have come to value those "feminine behaviors" in men and women unequally.

We see here that the students are faced with problems of being taught messages which are ahead of their time. In a world in which men and women accept women in positions of authority, humanism could be accepted by the female ministry students rather than regarded by them with ambivalence. In addition, if men and women were to participate equally in family care, the humanistic ideology would be appropriate for maintaining women's commitment to the ministry rather than being used by them as a rationale for quitting. In anticipating how they will justify their encumbency of the ministerial role to parishioners and interweave interpersonal and work involvements, the women realistically accommodate the more traditional messages of the outside world. Because the wider public "lags behind" the humanistic rhetoric, some of the female students use that rhetoric in ways circumscribed by old cultural understandings and adjust to that wider context by reverting back to old ways.

7

Conclusions

What is striking in the literature on professional socialization is students' *lack* of dilemmas of professional identification (e.g., Bucher and Stelling 1977). How is this so?

First, it is possible that in other professions, clients and professionals have the same expectations for trainees, thereby removing a source of the students' dilemmas. But as Freidson has argued (1970a, 1970b), professionals and their clients are distinct groups with divergent interests in and understandings of what the profession should provide and how. In addition, even without deprofessionalization, professions and their publics may undergo dramatic or minor changes in their expectations for professional behavior. Although occupations that have achieved the honorific title of profession often present themselves to us as superior, uniform, and never changing, they are neither homogeneous nor static (Coe 1970; Larson 1977). Professions comprise multiple segments (Bucher and Strauss 1961; Jarvis 1976), some of which may, at a particular time, effect changes in their professional ideology, practitioner's role, and core activity that spread throughout the professional body. Client publics, too, are in process, sometimes modifying their conception of what they want from professionals. It is unlikely, then, that nonministerial students are free of conflicting demands.

Second, students in other professional schools may have little contact with clients and others outside the organization, thereby making any conflicting expectations irrelevant to their daily experiences. But since professional schools are not total institutions, students are unlikely to be that isolated.

The seminary case suggests that most important for creating students' dilemmas of professional identification was the faculty's failure to provide a convincing ideology and rhetoric to legitimate the professional authority and autonomy of the ministry. The faculty did not provide a clear and coherent image of the profession as a distinctive and special occupation. When students in other programs do learn a convincing rhetoric of professional authority, they may still anticipate clients' discrepant messages but are probably not very concerned about them. By providing a strong ideology of professional authority, faculty may, implicitly or explicitly, discount outsiders' expectations as merely the "unprofessional" views of lay people. Let us look in some detail at how the seminary faculty's attempts to provide a sense of professional specialness through an unpersuasive rhetoric produced students' ambivalence toward it and problems of professional identification.

THE HUMANISTIC RHETORIC

The students took on an ideology that is both egalitarian and personalistic. The egalitarian dimension of the ideology suggests that ministers are not the sole religious authority; others, too, may become experts. The personal dimension suggests that good ministers should use their whole selves when interacting with clients and with each other. Within this framework, what becomes distinctive about the ministry is the individual minister's subjectivity and personal style, or individual characteristics.

A convincing rhetoric of professional authority would make students feel they are developing a valued "real self." The ministry students did feel they were acquiring a "real self," but one that was characterized by idiosyncrasies rather than by shared notions of what a good professional is. Ministers could make individuation and subjectivity the distinguishing features of the collectivity, however ambiguously defined. But according to the egalitarian dimension, clients' idiosyncracies are as valid and valuable as the minister's. Since both professionals and clients are experts from this view, what is distinctive about the ministry is unclear.

Students learned to value personal style and subjectivity as a distinguishing mark of the profession, but they also learned a rhetoric of social control that was collective—"community." "Community," as faculty and administrators used it, suggests that students like, are liked by, and are like each other. Since personalism and individualism are part of the new creed, how do community and homogeneity fit in? Faculty put these two conceptions—individualism and collectivism—together in the following way. They argued that those who accept the personal-egalitarian ideology might differ in many ways, but they are the same (good) in important ways "underneath it all." The idea is that if students will look for others' "real selves," they will discover that each person is good. In other words, faculty taught students to make the most of their individual differences yet also to expect similarity and sympathy among themselves. If students can feel this bond, they should sense that the profession is distinctive and special, for the term "community" denotes a positive affective state and confers group identity. Students expected their colleagues and teachers to be like them in important ways, ways that were, according to the subjective part of their ideology, left up to them to figure out. Students did share a sense that the good person is one who discloses personal information, but faculty allowed students to invoke other criteria as well. Because faculty emphasized individualism and ambiguously defined what a good professional is, students came up with different definitions. They acquired ambiguous and idealistic expectations for their teachers' and peers' behavior and their own. They expected their teachers and peers to be like them in various ways and learned to care a lot about this similarity because it presumably provided the basis for what is professionally distinctive about the ministry. Students eventually found out that they did not all share the same criteria for community. Since "community" was the basis of their sense of a shared professional identity, discovering negative individual differences was tantamount to discovering that there was no clear idea of what makes the ministry a profession.

Nor did faculty provide students with a clear-cut notion of

what is religious. Although they taught students to no longer equate religion with traditional morality, it was unclear which ideas and behaviors were religious—and hence a property of the ministry—and which were not. The new ministerial role still includes an ethical dimension; ministers, candidates learned, should be good people. But how to be good (besides being open about oneself) was not spelled out. Students learned neither a series of situational behaviors nor a language that pertained exclusively to the religious. They were told, for example, that their calling is equal to others' callings, including low-status occupations. They were taught to use the word "ministering" to describe all callings, which suggested that their profession provides the perspective that informs all other occupations. This notion, however, still obscures the meaning of what is distinctively ministerial. And, as we have seen, the argument that one can minister in all ways gave some students a rationale for quitting the ministry and doing something else instead.

One of the main problems with the ministry's new ideology of professional authority is its insistence that clients' views are as valid as professionals'. Students, in taking on this personal-egalitarian ideology, also learned to take the traditional view seriously. Faculty taught students to care about the views of parishioners, parents, friends, and others who often had traditional expectations of them. The personalizing part of the ideology suggests that students care about others' expectations. Students could not then simply discount parishioners' views as unprofessional. Consequently, they acquired an ambivalent professional identity, trying to accommodate both sets of expectations. In addition, by making clients' views credible, students worried about legitimating themselves as humanistic ministers (as professionals without professional authority) to clients who hold traditional expectations for professionals and conventional notions of professional authority. The female students were especially concerned about encountering such legitimation problems.

It is understandable that the students found outsiders' traditional views appealing—it gave them a clear basis of authority the program failed to provide and at the same time allowed them to feel they were, as humanists are supposed to, taking clients' views seriously.

Professional programs, then, probably prevent their students from developing the dilemmas discussed here by providing an authoritative image of professional authority. Thus it is understandable that medical students, nursing students, and graduate students are more concerned with "psyching out" their teachers, "fronting," and "making the grade" than these ministry students (see Becker et al. 1961; Haas and Shaffir 1977; Olesen and Whittaker 1968; Sanford 1976). Students in other schools take on a "cloak of professionalism," learning to appear as experts to their teachers even when they are not. Students in these schools learn to think of their profession as distinctive and admired. During professional socialization, the symbols and power of the profession are clear and the rhetoric of professionalism convincing. Because of that power, neophytes spend time proving themselves worthy of membership in the profession rather than figuring out if there is a profession to speak of. Students learn that if they wish to become professionals they must play the game, learn to please their professors, and act like they know more than they do. Hence, students become very concerned with performance in school and are hardly at all concerned with clients' views.

The absence of psyching-out and fronting behavior among the ministry students is striking. It can be explained by the absence of a strong ideology of professional authority and by the presence of the humanistic rhetoric. Given an ideology that comes close to being antiprofessional, students are not preoccupied with displaying competence. In the seminary, students are deemed fit for the professional role to the extent that they show *role distance* from a concern with competence or performance. Students do care about whether they will become good ministers, but in the seminary this is less a matter of displaying one's skills and knowledge than in being the "right kind of person." They show they are the right kind of people by displaying their individuality, spontaneity, and "gut feelings" rather than technical skills. Students are more likely to "front" when they interact with parishioners from their home town, for they learn to care that that audience expects them to show signs of omnipotence and omniscience.

Socialization as Identification
and Division

> In pure identification there would be no strife. Like-
> wise, there would be no strife in absolute separateness,
> since opponents can join battle only through a media-
> tory ground that makes their communication possible,
> thus providing the first condition necessary for their in-
> terchange of blows. But put identification and division
> ambiguously together, so that you cannot know for cer-
> tain just where one ends and the other beings, and you
> have the characteristic invitation to rhetoric.
>
> Kenneth Burke, *A Rhetoric of Motives*

The ministry responded to deprofessionalization by putting
identification and division together—they tried to create a sense
of distinctiveness (division, in Burke's terms) through identifying
their tasks (role, religion, rhetoric), with a secular culture that had
put the authority of the profession into question. By so doing, the
ministers made what is distinctive and special about the ministry
ambiguous. This filters down to the level of the seminary, where
students receive conflicting messages.

Is the balancing of identification and division among socializers
and their charges a problem that characterizes socialization generally? At the onset of socialization, socializing agents and their
charges constitute separate groups, often of unequal status and
knowledge. They are, then, initially divided. In order for socialization to take place, socializing agents must try to identify their
interests with those of recruits—that is, recruits must think that
socializers have their best interests at heart. Once this occurs, recruits are likely to trust their socializers' demands and become the
kind of people socializers expect them to be. In addition, socializers
may try to get recruits to identify with them. For example, in professional schools, recruits are usually expected to identify with the
professional group by the time they leave the organization. Socialization, particularly when it is largely voluntary, is a time when
identification and division constitute a shifting relationship, not a
dichotomy. That is recruits and their socializing agents are neither purely identified nor absolutely separated. Although the two

groups are divided in some respects, recruits are supposed to become like their socializers, hence producing a situation in which
identification and division are equivocally combined.

Burke argues that such ambiguity invites the use of rhetoric.
Socializing agents and recruits are able to use the rhetoric of the
organization to produce identification or division, bringing about
constant shifts from one to the other. By this I mean the following: Socializers may use their rhetoric to get recruits to believe
that they and socializers are united (producing identification); yet,
recruits may also use their socializers' rhetoric to question or resist
the latter's demands (producing division). Rhetoric, then, is central to socialization and helps us understand its problematic nature.

The Construction of Identification and Division

Burke notes that people sometimes identify themselves with
others when their interests are joined. Alternatively, a person, A,

> may *identify himself* with B even when their interests are not joined, if he
> assumes that they are, or is persuaded to believe so. (Burke 1962, 544)

I have discussed one way socializers deal—perhaps unsuccess-
fully—with the tension between identification and division. Socializers can create identification between themselves and recruits
by using ambiguous words that recruits already value.

What do I mean by ambiguous? I do not mean that certain
words are inherently more unclear than others. Rather, people of
one society (or subsociety) may use a particular word in quite specific ways, while people of another society may be less restrictive
in their usage. I adopt the view that because all language is symbolic, it is fundamentally open and uncertain (Duncan 1968;
Winterowd 1968, 4–8). As Cohen put it: "Symbols are objects,
acts, concepts, or linguistic formations that stand *ambiguously* for
a multiplicity of disparate meanings, evoke sentiments and emotions, and impel men to action" (1974, ix; emphasis in original).
Because of the symbolic nature of language, people can increase
or decrease the ambiguity of words, depending on their purposes.
Consequently,

> Meaning . . . is always a variable, ranging between nonsense, on the one
> hand—the total absence of coincident responses—and what might be

called boredom on the other—the total coincidence of such responses. (Stone 1970, 396)

If socializers use a rhetoric consisting of conventionally ambiguous yet valued words (such as democracy, freedom, community), they may obscure differences between themselves and recruits that the latter might find important and disturbing. By glossing over divisions between people, socializers can use rhetoric as a basis for producing "intersubjectivity" (Schutz 1970), or the belief people have that they share understanding. In hearing socializers use appealing words which mean all things to all people, recruits may assume identification with them (Brembeck and Howell 1952, 145). Consequently, recruits will probably trust their socializers and comply with their demands, especially if socializers use the rhetoric to justify their demands.

However, while the use of ambiguous words, particularly those that appeal to many, may make people think they agree upon what those words mean, it may also have the opposite effect. Those socialized may discover that the words or language they share in fact mask differences in meaning or message. Adler alluded to this double-edged potential of rhetoric in her study of an art school:

At first, this ambiguity [of the radical rhetoric] facilitated the Institute's simultaneous appeal to different groups, helping to mask and hold in abeyance their conflicting values and interests, but it soon proved unstable. (1979, 44)

Once this happens, recruits may think socializers use the rhetoric as a cliché or as a means of social control. If socializers have used words that reflect values, recruits are likely to care deeply about the discrepancies in meaning. Depending on the circumstance, they may leave the organization. If they stay, they may challenge organizational demands and violate at times even the basic (shared) expectations implied by the ambiguous rhetoric. In short, they may come to question whether the organization deserves their commitment. However, since they value the rhetoric, they do not simply act "deviant" but feel they must justify their actions to themselves and others. Since the words of the rhetoric are ambiguous, recruits find that they can use them to challenge others for not living up to the ideals and to justify their own acts which violate the expectations associated with the rhetoric.

THE PROBLEMATIC NATURE OF SOCIALIZATION

I have suggested that socialization is inherently problematic because it always involves the use of symbols, the meanings of which
are often equivocal. The ambiguity of language is a variable, for
no symbol is absolutely constraining for everyone who under-
stands it.

How else might socialization be problematic? This study suggests that different people, at different times, offer varying degrees
of both "value embracement" and behavioral conformity. Recruits
may accept the ideals, but reject their socializers' demands, or vice
versa. Following Merton, Rosow noted the importance of differ-
ential patterns of socialization. He argued that there are four "socialization types," each one varying on the dimensions of value
adoption and behavioral conformity:

> The fully *Socialized* has both the values and the behavior [of socializing
> agents]. The *Dilettante* is committed to the values, but does not perform
> adequately for viable group membership or acceptable role fulfillment.
> . . . The *Chameleon* is competent, skilled and actively meets behavioral
> expectations. But his conformity is essentially adaptive, without the cor-
> responding value basis on which the behavior presumably rests. . . . The
> *Unsocialized* neither has the beliefs nor displays adequate performance.
> (1965, 36)

My data indicate, however, that people may move from one type
to another. Further, Rosow places the rebel in the unsocialized
category, implying that those who challenge the system reject the
values of their socializing agents. Those being socialized who
cling most strongly to the ideals of their socializers may also offer
the most resistance. Idealists are most likely to care about discrepancies between ideals and reality. This produces the following paradox of socialization: Those who become most socialized to the
ideals are least likely to conform. There is a further irony—these
"oversocialized" people may become disillusioned and drop out,
hence ridding the system of some of its troublemakers.

This brings us to a fundamental problem of adult socialization
and probably childhood socialization as well: Those being socialized may turn the substance of their socialization back upon their
socializing agents. This goes further than Clausen's point that
"deviant behaviors as well as conforming behaviors are learned in

the course of any individual's socialization experience" (1966, 250). Those being socialized may use socializers' ideals to produce or justify deviance. Recruits may argue that socializing agents do not live up to the ideals they espouse, or that the world does not match the picture socializers have painted of it. We have seen both types of resistance in the seminary. Students sometimes used the organizational rhetoric to challenge socializers for claiming that they and recruits constituted a community. Consequently, recruits sometimes challenged organizational demands made in the name of the community rhetoric. In addition, recruits could use the rhetoric socializing agents provided to justify their own violations of the norms of the community. Sociologists have in general ignored this dimension of recruits' control over their socialization, that is, the possibility of their turning what they have learned from their teachers against their teachers. One of the exceptions is Ball, who suggested that sarcasm can be used by the controlled as well as by the controllers:

Sarcasm may also be utilized as a technique for impairing or destroying control and stability, by deflating or debasing the controller or in some other way encouraging a state of disequilibrium. Thus, sarcasm as control may be a two-edged sword, at the disposal of the controlled as well as the controllers. (1965, 195)

Similarly, as Ball points out (ibid., 196), Scheler's (1961) notion of ressentiment implies that those being controlled can turn the values of their controllers against them. Future research could explore how recruits, individually and collectively, learn to use their teachers' messages for their own purposes.

Sociologists often assume that socializing messages are clear and that all the researcher has to do is find out who accepts the messages and who does not. I have already suggested that the relationship of message to conformity (or value to behavior) is problematic. I wish to add that socializers sometimes communicate their messages in an ambiguous way, whether intentionally or unwittingly. In other words, the content of socialization may be difficult to delineate. At Midwest Seminary, socializing agents used words from the traditional rhetoric to convince recruits to accept humanistic messages and organizational demands. Consequently, it was often difficult for recruits to know what socializers were "really" trying to say. Also, the messages may be complex and even contradictory. Instructional personnel at the seminary communicated a message which implied that recruits should heed others' expectations which contradicted their own. We might deal with this complexity by finding out what socializing agents say they wish to communicate, how they convey their messages, and what the recruits' interpretations are. My data show that socializers may obfuscate their messages in order to legitimate them. This self-defeating endeavor is nevertheless one explanation for why recruits often misconstrue what their socializers are trying to teach them. Future research should discover the complexity of what socializers convey.

Socializers sometimes try to communicate ambiguity as content. For example, humanistic professionals teach a role that is supposed to be fairly open or "roleless." Although we know that expectations are always mobilized by identity, these socializers seem to be emphasizing form over content. Put differently, the main content of these agents' teaching is form, that is, style of interaction. Future research might compare the socialization process in these settings with those in which content is emphasized over form.

What students learn may be complicated further by the expectations held by people outside the socializing setting (see Olesen and Whittaker 1970). Relevant audiences or reference groups may interfere with what socializers are trying to do, especially if the organization is not a total institution. In the seminary, the expectations of recruits' parents, relatives, and home-town friends were largely discrepant with those of their teachers. I argued that such discrepancies need not interfere, but that socializers may make them relevant. We might study the ways in which audiences outside the organization gain or lose their relevance to the socialization process over time.

Future research might also focus on the kinds of discrepancies insiders and outsiders bring to the socialization experience of recruits. This study suggests one type of problem—some agents socialize recruits for tomorrow, while others ratify the messages of yesterday.

METHODOLOGICAL APPENDIX

This Appendix has three parts: a brief history of the project, a discussion of how field workers might gain rapport with respondents in similar settings, and a discussion of research problems that arise when respondents' words and way of talking resemble sociological jargon and theorizing.

A HISTORY OF THE PROJECT

How did the project begin? In my second year of graduate study in sociology at the University of Minnesota, I decided to take a field work course in sociology at another university in the midwest. I did not plan to study Midwest Seminary, or any seminary, before moving from Minneapolis in January of 1978 to the town in which the university is located. I had corresponded with the instructor, who suggested that I choose a field site after I arrived.

A section of the Methodological Appendix was published in Sherryl Kleinman, "Learning the Ropes as Field Work Analysis," in *Field Work Experience: Qualitative Approaches to Social Research*, edited by William B. Shaffir, Robert A. Stebbins, and Allan Turowetz, pp. 171–83. Copyright © 1980 by St. Martin's Press, Inc. Reprinted by permission of the publisher.

A graduate student at the host university (a friend of a friend) offered to help me find housing for the ten-week period. A few weeks before the course began, she told me that a room was available at a dormitory in a seminary located on the university's campus. I was so relieved at the thought of having somewhere to stay and in such a convenient location that I didn't think about the kind of place it might be until I was on my way. At that time, I reflected on what living in a seminary might be like and worried a little about it. I expected students, for instance, to pray much of the time, wear black, look sombre, read the Bible a lot, talk about theology, God, personal faith, and perhaps proselytize. Most of my colleagues also presumed that seminaries are (or should be) pervaded by religious behavior and talk. Upon hearing that I would be living in a seminary, most of my friends and colleagues laughed and said, "*You* are going to live in a seminary?!" They thought that someone who is at best agnostic could not live in a seminary and "take it." However, my happiness at finding otherwise ideal living quarters outweighed my fears. I told myself that I could probably take it for the duration of the course.

I arrived at the dormitory the day before the class started and met some of the ministry students. Given the questions people have when they move somewhere and the need to have them answered, I found myself treating the students as people who could give me, a new dorm dweller, information. I asked them where certain facilities were located, such as the cafeteria and laundry room, and what the surrounding area offered in the way of stores and restaurants. In retrospect, it is surprising that I was able to treat them primarily as dorm dwellers rather than as ministry students. If I had thought about it, I probably would have found other people to answer my questions. However, given the initial feelings of disorientation I experienced at being in a new town, residence, and university, I was able, to some degree, to put aside the stereotype of "religious people" that would have stood in the way of getting my questions answered. I did not, however, forget that they were ministry students. Rather, during these encounters, I was struck by how "normal" they seemed. They looked and talked like students generally, not ministry students. For example, I noticed that only two or three students bowed their heads in prayer before meals in the seminary cafeteria. I wondered, "What's wrong with the others? Surely, one doesn't have to be very religious to say grace!" Clearly their behavior and appearance violated my expectations of religious people, and I thought, surely ministry students are representative members of that category!

I was intrigued by the discrepancies—how could my expectations be so off the mark? After getting settled in my room, I asked two female students how they and others might feel about me studying them. I explained that this would entail hanging around with them as much as possible and conducting interviews. They seemed excited about the prospect and speculated that others would react similarly. Heartened by their enthusiasm, and having heard a rumor that the instructor of the field work class would demand that a field site be chosen by the end of the first class, I decided to try it.

As Geer (1967) points out, field workers' surprises in their first days in the field often highlight their implicit working hypotheses. For example, my initial reactions to the students indicated that I expected ministry students to act more like ministers than students. The students I first met did not act as "religiously" as I expected them to (at least where I observed them), producing a number of questions: Do most of these students act more like students than ministers or just the few that I have met? Is my reaction of surprise idiosyncratic, reflective of my background, or would anyone react similarly? If one can reasonably expect to find religious behavior in a seminary, then how can I account for its absence? Does religious behavior go on in certain places with certain people in the setting, places I do not yet have (or may not get) access to? If so, where, with whom, and why not in plain view? These were not my only questions, but the ones that occupied me the most at the time.

As students and I befriended each other, I found myself spending a lot of their and my leisure time with them. I ate meals with the students and spent time with them in the evenings and in-between classes. It was at these times that students joked about religion and others' religious expectations of them. Other data which suggested that conventional religion was absent, or at least in short supply at this seminary, came from the students' acceptance of me. Since I am Jewish and agnostic, I expected the students to treat me like an outsider. However, my notes indicate that the students not only accepted me, but took me into their confidence almost immediately. For example, on the fourth day of field work, the following occurred:

During supper in the cafeteria, Marge said, "Hey, Sherryl, do you want to see *A Star Is Born*? It's playing at University Theatre for a dollar. We're going to the 7 o'clock show." I said, "Sure." . . . I met Marge and Vivian in the dorm lounge at 6:45. On the way over to the film Marge said, "Are you really just here for a quarter?" I said, "Yes, probably." Marge said, "You can't just extend it? I'm getting used to you." Marge and Debbie laughed. Marge continued, "Even though you're an observer we think of you as more than that. I mean, you're not in the seminary, but you're *with* us." (Field notes)

However, I was also conducting open-ended interviews and found that the students became quite serious about religion during these encounters. As time progressed, I noted that although these students did not talk much about theology or their faith in public they did not sound like "any students." Their analytic-moralistic talk about whether their peers and teachers were acting like good people contrasted with, for example, the pragmatic, making-the-grade talk of undergraduates (Becker et al., 1968). Further, their terminology seemed to be a mixture of religion and psychology. For example, "theologizing" largely meant talking about interpersonal relations, often with little or no mention of God. The question "Are these students 'really' religious?" was becoming more complicated.

Since students used this mixed terminology to talk about their classes, it seemed likely that they had picked it up from their professors. I therefore started to attend classes (trying to go to some in each area), chapel services, and special functions and interviewed some members of the faculty. Since one of the administrators was especially involved in changing the curriculum, I interviewed him (as well as another key administrator). I had already decided to focus on the ministry students. The classes and interviews with socializers revealed the organizational demands and expectations that helped explain students' behavior and identity.

After about four weeks, the instructor of the field work course suggested that I stay at least one more term, possibly gathering enough data for a dissertation. During the second term, I focused on activities in the main seminary building (where classes and chapel services are held) and continued to hang around with students outside of class. At the end of the second term (which was also the end of the academic year), I decided to return for at least one month during the fall of the next academic year. I especially wanted to be at the seminary during orientation, when the new cohort arrives. I went back to the seminary for orientation a week before classes began and spent another four weeks there.

RESEARCH PROBLEMS

Since there are various types of theological schools (Carroll 1971), I cannot make any definitive statements about how to do field work in seminaries. However, I will comment on one of the potential problems of studying "ideological organizations" and offer a possible solution.

Before studying an organization to which ideology is conventionally defined as central, we anticipate that respondents will be overcommitted to their beliefs. We assume that these people, unlike others, cannot effect role distance but are engulfed by their role. Consequently, we treat respondents as if the status they hold in the organization is their only identity. In some seminaries (or in other so-called ideological organizations) respondents may in fact live as if the one identity were their only one. However, at Midwest Seminary and probably at other humanistically oriented theological schools, students tried to resist others' placement of them in the ministerial identity. In short, they experienced the pervasiveness of the identity as a constraint. In order to gain rapport, it might be helpful (as it was for me) to give respondents the opportunities to assume a variety of identities when interacting with them. As I pointed out earlier, I at first treated some of the students as dorm dwellers (out of personal, rather than research interests). Further, when the students discussed matters in ways that didn't seem appropriately ministerial, I tried to participate as I might have with friends who were not ministers. I found it helpful, then, to make or let the students make several of my identities relevant to the research.

These identities were of two types. The first type included identities that I shared with some respondents, such as resident of the midwest, dorm dweller, woman, student. Shared identification provided common ground and things to talk about during initial encounters. Further, because students, for the most part, valued these identities, shared identification also aided the development of trust. The second type included identities I did not share with the respondents but which became relevant, such as Canadian and Jew. I discovered that these identities, precisely because they were different but unthreatening, aroused the students' curiosity and provided me with something to offer them—interesting stories. This process of using our identities in interaction with respondents is not unique to field work but is characteristic of normal conversation; we make the most of our similarities and differences with others to secure and maintain a level of interest and to achieve rapport.

Student was probably my most important shared identity. Most of the respondents had been students for most of their lives (about as long as I had) and were still in that status. Also, although ministerial students learn different things than sociology students, students generally share many routines, relationships, and understandings. Respondents could, for example, talk to me about classes, exams, professors, and grades, knowing that I had more than a vague understanding of what they were talking about or doing. (I did, of course, have to learn the particular ways in which these situations, events, and people took on significance for them.) Therefore, being a student was important because it offered shared knowledge as well as shared identification.

Given the general stereotype of ministers and ministry students as people who are, above all else, religious, I presupposed that Jew would become an important identity in the setting. I also anticipated that this would be a negative identity—they might think that only a Christian could really understand what goes on in their seminary. It turned out that this identity did not even become relevant for a while, since they could not tell I was Jewish. When they did ask questions about my religious background, being Jewish became an asset. Most of the students had had little contact with Jews and equated being Jewish with being a religious Jew. They were quite interested to learn that Jewish people differ in degree of religiosity and life style. Further, I have no evidence to indicate that they thought my religious identity would interfere with my ability to do the study.

By bringing a number of identities into the interaction, both respondents and researchers get to know each other better and learn to feel comfortable in each other's presence. Also, by broadening the range of relevant identities, I acquired data I might not have gotten otherwise. For example, in letting respondents know that my interest in them as ministry students did not preclude an interest in their other identities, students thought it reasonable to include me in their leisure activities and tell me about interpersonal relationships. Further, in this setting, treating the respondents as people who hold many identities helped me achieve rapport because I was granting them a right which many outsiders deny them—the right to act like regular people.

I do not mean to suggest that none of a field worker's identities will interfere with the research process or alienate respondents. Some familiar identities may bring out an old contempt just as an alien identity might produce an immediate response of distrust. Fortunately, in one sense, the researcher is likely to find out about these identities soon enough and can therefore try to deal with the conflict. Respondents, like field workers, can change their preconceptions, but because we have a greater interest in developing empathy than they do, it is up to us to convince them that we are not really that bad. For example, a few of my respondents had taken some sociology courses as undergraduates and had in the process acquired a rather negative view of the field and its practitioners. They would, off and on, make snide remarks to me about being a sociologist. I decided to confront them about this and probe their attitudes. These students shared a positivistic conception of the field and felt that I would purposefully avoid taking their perspective into account. Their distrust and remarks subsided after I explained to them that I was using a sociological framework which made their meanings central.

I am not suggesting that researchers bring every identity to initial or later encounters. If there is good reason to believe that particular information might alienate respondents and can easily be kept out of the interaction then it is probably best not to reveal it. Field workers should exercise some caution in deciding what to reveal at the outset because certain identities will tend to stick with them throughout the research; others will only become relevant on a few occasions.

PROBLEMS OF ANALYSIS:
RESPONDENTS AS SOCIAL PSYCHOLOGISTS

Community

Much of the students' terminology and theorizing was similar to the sociologist's. For example, they often used the words "role," "self," "identity," and especially "community." In any field study, there is the danger that researchers may be seduced by respondents' questions, and use them instead of our own. When respondents' questions sound sociological, it is even more difficult to distinguish between ours and theirs. For example, students were concerned about creating community in the seminary, and about the mechanisms which would make community work or break down. These concerns are also sociological questions, as Kanter (1972) has shown. Consequently, I found myself moving in the direction of adopting the students' questions rather than treating them as data. I did not at that time ask "How is it that these students are concerned with 'community'?" or "What are the consequences of this concern for their everyday life at the seminary?" Also, by adopting the students' questions, I took for granted that they had a precise meaning for community.

Thinking that I might do a community study, I read some of the sociological literature in the area and discovered that sociologists used that word in many different ways. At the same time, my data indicated that students also meant different things by their words. Moreover, now and then, students discovered that their meanings differed and they would get upset about it. Because both sociologists and students used the word in so many ways, I found that I could not just define it and get on with the problem of discovering when community worked and when it did not. Given the confusion, I tried to develop codes for students' and faculty's various meanings, finding that community sometimes referred to activities of different kinds, or units of social organization (friendship groups, the seminary) or affect (spirit of community). I noticed that students' usages resembled sociological usages, which made me wonder whether sociologists, too, had not clearly delineated the phenomenon.

I then came across Joseph Gusfield's *Community: A Critical Response* (1975) and Raymond Plant's *Community and Ideology* (1974). They suggested that sociologists have used the word "community" evaluatively as well as descriptively, usually to indicate their notion of the good or bad society. These readings, together with my data, led me to focus on community as one of my respondents' folk constructs—part of the apparatus of their society—which should be studied sociologically.

I then wanted to know where students used the word and from whom they had picked it up. I noted that instructional personnel often used the word in classes, especially during self-disclosure sessions and in sermons in the chapel. I also noticed its presence in such documents as the course catalog, newletters, and ministry projects.

I stopped looking for what community "really" meant and focused instead on when and how faculty, administrators, and students used the word. Everyone used it and seemed to take its meaning for granted, but it was not clear to me that everyone really agreed. I observed that (1) community was used in many ways, (2) students often assumed they all meant the same thing by the word, and (3) students became upset when they thought others violated community expectations or did not share the same expectations for community.

It did not seem right that students and faculty could use the word in so many ways. As a field worker and a symbolic interactionist (Blumer 1969), I had been trained to take respondents' words seriously. Since respondents used one word often, I expected its salience to indicate something important about their daily life. However, if one looks at some field workers' accounts of respondents' talk, such as the argot of roles in prison (Sykes 1958) or the term "crock" in medical school (Becker et al. 1961), particular words come to have particular meanings in particular settings. I expected that the meaning of community would become obvious, too. For example, in the case of the "crock," the researchers pointed out that eventually they, like their respondents, could point to a medical case and know if it was a crock, or something else. Community, on the other hand, did not have clear referents; its central characteristic was its ambiguity and the fact that faculty and students valued it.

The meanings of community were many, but the function of the word was more specific. Community, as an ambiguous word with traditional and moral appeal could be used by the faculty, as well as by the students, to make claims on others. In short, community was used as a rhetoric to convince others to have certain beliefs or to engage in certain actions. Faculty could get students to do things they might otherwise have resisted by (1) using community as a "mystification" and (2) linking community to recruits' "real selves." Community served as a mystification in that the faculty's usage obscured differences between recruits that might have produced conflict (Burke 1962, 625–34). Students presumed identification, making it easier for them to trust their socializers' demands. Further, because faculty linked community to the "real selves" of recruits, they made conformity to demands made in the name of community an important matter, arguing that only the "community person" could become a good minister. Students, however, could also use the term to get what they wanted and to question discrepancies between the ideal and the reality of seminary life. They, too, could use the word to mystify—to justify the divisions (such as segregation between whites and blacks) which violate "community." Both faculty and students could use the word for rhetorical purposes.

To summarize, I first assumed that students and I shared a sociological conception of community and a research question about when community works. I then relinquished this assumption and focused instead on the word as a datum and tried to find out why students were so concerned about community. In doing so, I noted that community did not have a fixed meaning in the organization. Also, I could see that while people sometimes did not mean the same thing when they used the word in interaction, they often were unaware of it. In finding out how this could happen, I discovered that people often used the word for rhetorical purposes.

Role

Although students also used the term "role," a word which is as much a part of sociological jargon as "community," it was easier to distinguish between sociological and common-sense usages. Interestingly, I noted that students used role when referring to traditional, but not humanistic, expectations of ministers. Students recognized the social dimension of the traditional role, but not of the humanistic role. Students, for example, could see that people placed them in the identity of minister, expecting them to act in certain ways. They were sociological realists about their situation vis-à-vis clients, parents, and old friends. They were, however, sociologically naive about the new role, believing that one could be roleless or just be "a self." This is the humanistic message regarding role—one should obliterate the role and allow one's "true self" to emerge. These contrasting usages highlighted sociological differences between humanistic and traditional roles.

Students' Theorizing

I also had to distinguish between social-psychological theorizing and students' analyses. Like psychotherapists, these students learned to "perform and to theorize about social interaction in a new way" (Blum and Rosenberg 1968, 82). In short, they treated social interaction as a matter of theoretic rather than practical interest. The students' talk more closely resembled "scientific theorizing" than common-sense knowledge (see Garfinkel 1967).

Students at Midwest Seminary had a self-consciousness and other-awareness that is much less common in "practical" interactions. They often analyzed interpersonal relationships, formulating quasi-social scientific analyses of behavior. Given my interest in self-conception and identity, it was at first difficult to keep my analyses separate from theirs. I dealt with this problem by looking at how their talk differed from sociological theorizing and making their talk central to the analysis.

Contrary to the canons of social science, students' talk was supposed to be evaluative. They considered treating people as ob-

jects of theoretical interest immoral. Instead, they made judg-
ments about how caring their teachers and peers were. Their
analyses, then, approximated what one might call moral-scientific
theorizing.

Students' talk provided data about their socialization. For example, their theorizing could be understood by the kinds of messages they received from faculty and administrators. Instructional
personnel made interpersonal relations a value and expected students to participate in changing themselves and others in the
organization. These messages made students acutely aware of
themselves and others, particularly in the context of interpersonal
relations. In addition to focusing on content, I also made talk central by looking for its function in the organization. In this case it
was rhetorical.

In order to apply the symbolic-interactionist perspective to field
work methodology, we must make "the meanings that things have
for [respondents] central in their own right" (Blumer 1969, 3).
However, in using this approach, we may be seduced by respondents' questions, especially if they seem sociological. We want to
give full consideration to respondents' concerns and concepts, and
in so doing we may let their analysis become ours.

Perhaps most researchers adopt respondents' questions and
concerns in the early stages of field work because they learn about
the setting while establishing rapport and gaining empathy. If respondents' talk at that time sounds sociological, researchers may
be especially vulnerable to adopting their respondents' questions.

I suggest that researchers make explicit their sense that respondents are doing sociological work. They might then ask, How is
respondents' language similar to or different from the sociologist's? Where have respondents learned to make interaction (or
"community," "role," and so on) a matter of theoretic rather than
practical interest? What can respondents do in their theorizing
that social scientists cannot (and vice versa) and why? What is the
function of respondents' "sociological" language? By addressing
these questions, respondents' language becomes data, and our
language becomes a tool for analyzing theirs.

REFERENCES

Adler, Judith E. 1979. *Artists in Offices: An Ethnography of an Academic Art Scene*. New Brunswick, N.J. Transaction books.

Ball, Donald W. 1965. "Sarcasm as Sociation: The Rhetoric of Interaction." *Canadian Review of Sociology and Anthropology* 2:190–98.

Becker, Howard S. 1970. "The Nature of a Profession." In *Sociological Work: Method and Substance*, edited by H. S. Becker, 87–103. Chicago: Aldine.

Becker, Howard S., Blanche Geer, and Everett C. Hughes. 1968. *Making the Grade: The Academic Side of College Life*. New York: Wiley.

Becker, Howard S., Blanche Geer, Everett C. Hughes, and Anselm Strauss. 1961. *Boys in White: Student Culture in Medical School*. Chicago: University of Chicago Press.

Bell, Daniel. 1977. "The Return of the Sacred? The Argument on the Future of Religion." *British Journal of Sociology* 28:419–48.

Bellah, Robert N. 1964. "Religious Evolution." *American Sociological Review* 29:358–74.

Bennett, Judith Deutsch. 1965. "The Would-be Architect: A Study of Social Factors Relating to Success and Failure in Occupational Choice." Master's thesis. University of Minnesota.

Berger, Peter L. 1979. *The Heretical Imperative*. Garden City, N.Y.: Anchor Press.

Blizzard, Samuel. 1958. "The Protestant Parish Minister's Integrating Roles." *Religious Education* 53:374–80.

Blum, Alan F., and Larry Rosenberg. 1968. "Some Problems Involved in Professionalizing Social Interaction: The Case of Psychotherapeutic Training." *Journal of Health and Social Behavior* 9:72–85.

Blumer, Herbert. 1969. *Symbolic Interactionism*. Englewood Cliffs, N.J.: Prentice-Hall.

Boulding, Elise. 1977. *Women in the Twentieth-Century World*. Beverly Hills, Ca.: Sage.

Bourne, Patricia G., and Norma J. Wikler. 1978. "Commitment and the Cultural Mandate: Women in Medicine." *Social Problems* 25:430–40.

Brembeck, Winston L., and William S. Howell. 1952. *Persuasion: A Means of Social Control*. Englewood Cliffs, N.J.: Prentice-Hall.

Bucher, Rue, and Joan G. Stelling. 1977. *Becoming Professional*. Beverly Hills, Ca.: Sage.

Bucher, Rue, and Anselm Strauss. 1961. "Professions in Process." *American Journal of Sociology* 66:325–34.

Burke, Kenneth. 1962. *A Rhetoric of Motives*. Cleveland: World Publishing Co.

Carroll, Jackson Walker. 1971. "Structural Effects of Professional Schools on Professional Socialization: The Case of Protestant Clergymen." *Social Forces* 50:61–74.

Charlton, Joy. 1978. "Women Entering the Ordained Ministry: Contradictions and Dilemmas of Status." Manuscript.

Clausen, John A. 1966. "Research on Socialization and Personality Development in the United States and France: Remarks on the Paper by Professor Chombart de Lauwe." *American Sociological Review* 31:248–57.

Coe, Rodney M. 1970. "Processes in the Development of Established Professions." *Journal of Health and Social Behavior* 11:59–67.

Cohen, Abner. 1974. *Two-dimensional Man: An Essay on the Anthropology of Power and Symbolism in Complex Society*. London: Routledge and Kegan Paul.

Douglas, Ann. 1977. *The Feminization of American Culture*. New York: Avon.

Duncan, Hugh Dalziel. 1968. *Symbols in Society*. New York: Oxford University Press.

Ebaugh, Helen Rose Fuchs. 1977. *Out of the Cloister: A Study of Organizational Dilemmas*. Austin, Texas: University of Texas Press.

Freidson, Eliot. 1970a. *Professional Dominance*. Chicago: Aldine.

———. 1970b. *Profession of Medicine*. New York: Dodd-Mead.

Fukayama, Yoshio. 1972. *The Ministry in Transition: A Case Study of Theological Education*. University Park: Pennsylvania State University Press.

Garfinkel, Harold. 1967. *Studies in Ethnomethodology*. Englewood Cliffs, N.J.: Prentice-Hall.

Garrett, William R. 1973. "Politicized Clergy: A Sociological Interpretation of the 'New Breed.'" *Journal for the Scientific Study of Religion* 12:383–99.

Geer, Blanche. 1967. "First Days in the Field." In *Sociologists at Work*, edited by Phillip E. Hammond, 372–98. Garden City, N.Y.: Doubleday.

Gilkey, Langdon. 1967. "Social and Intellectual Sources of Contemporary Protestant Theology in America." *Daedalus* 96:69–98.

Gilligan, Carol. 1982. *In a Different Voice: Psychological Theory and Moral Development*. Cambridge: Harvard University Press.

Glaser, Barney G., and Anselm L. Strauss. 1967. *The Discovery of Grounded Theory*. Chicago: Aldine.

Goffman, Erving. 1961. *Asylums*. Garden City, N.Y.: Doubleday.

Goldner, F. H., T. P. Ference, and R. R. Ritti. 1973. "Priests and Laity: A Profession in Transition." In *Professionalisation and Social Change*, edited by P. Halmos, 119–37. Sociological Review Monograph no. 20. Staffordshire: University of Keele.

Greeley, Andrew M. 1972. *The Denominational Society: A Sociological Approach to Religion in America*. Glenview, Ill.: Scott, Foresman.

Gusfield, Joseph. 1975. *Community: A Critical Response*. New York: Harper and Row.

Gustavus, W. T. 1973. "The Ministerial Student: A Study in the Contradictions of a Marginal Role." *Review of Religious Research* 3:187–93.

Haas, Jack, and William Shaffir. 1977. "The Professionalization of Medical Students: Developing Competence and a Cloak of Competence." *Symbolic Interaction* 1:71–88.

Hadden, Jeffrey K. 1969. *The Gathering Storm in the Churches*. Garden City, N.Y.: Doubleday.

Hadden, S. C., and M. Lester. 1978. "Talking Identity: The Production of 'Self' in Interaction." *Human Studies* 1:331–56.

Halmos, Paul. 1966. *The Faith of the Counsellors*. New York: Basic Books.

———. 1970. *The Personal Service Society*. New York: Schocken.

———. 1978. *The Personal and the Political: Social Work and Political Action*. London: Hutchinson.

Hammersmith, Sue Kiefer. 1976. "Being a Nun: Social Order and Change in a Radical Community." Ph.D. dissertation, Indiana University.

Hammond, Judith M. 1980. "Biography Building to Insure the Future: Women's Negotiation of Gender Relevancy in Medical School." *Symbolic Interaction* 3:35–49.

Haug, Marie R. 1973. "Deprofessionalization: An Alternative Hypothesis for the Future." *Professionalisation and Social Change*, edited by P. Halmos, 195–211. Sociological Review Monograph no. 20. Staffordshire: University of Keele.

Haug, Marie R., and Marvin B. Sussman. 1969. "Professional Autonomy and the Revolt of the Client." *Social Problems* 17: 153–60.

Heilbrun, Carolyn G. 1979. *Reinventing Womanhood*. New York: Norton.

Hiller, Harry H. 1969. "The New Theology and the Sociology of Religion." *Canadian Review of Sociology and Anthropology* 6:179–87.

Hirschman, Albert O. 1970. *Exit, Voice, and Loyalty: Responses to Decline in Firms, Organizations, and States*. Cambridge, Mass.: Harvard University Press.

Hughes, Everett C. 1971. "Professions." In *The Sociological Eye*, edited by Everett C. Hughes, 376–86. Chicago: Aldine.

Jarvis, Peter. 1976. "A Profession in Process: A Theoretical Model for the Ministry." *Sociological Review* 24:351–64.

Kadushin, Charles. 1962. "Social Distance between Client and Professional." *American Journal of Sociology* 67:517–31.

Kanter, Rosabeth Moss. 1972. *Commitment and Community: Communes and Utopias in Sociological Perspective*. Cambridge, Mass.: Harvard University Press.

———. 1977. *Men and Women of the Corporation*. New York: Basic Books.

Katz, Jack. 1972. "Deviance, Charisma, and Rule-Defined Behavior." *Social Problems* 20:186–202.

Keniston, Kenneth. 1968. *Young Radicals: Notes on Committed Youth*. New York: Harcourt, Brace and World.

Larson, Magali Sarfatti. 1977. *The Rise of Professionalism*. Berkeley, Ca.: University of California Press.

Leat, Diana. 1973. "'Putting God Over': The Faithful Counsellors." *Sociological Review* 21:561–72.

Lemert, Charles. 1974a. "Cultural Multiplexity and Religious Polytheism." *Social Compass* 21(3):241–53.

———. 1974b. "Sociological Theory and the Relativistic Paradigm." *Sociological Inquiry* 44:93–104.

Lever, Janet. 1976. "Sex Differences in the Games Children Play." *Social Problems* 23:478–87.

Lipset, Seymour Martin, and Philip G. Albach. 1968. "The Quest for Community on Campus." In *The Search for Community in Modern America*, edited by E. Digby Baltzell, 123–47. New York: Harper and Row.

Luckmann, Thomas. 1967. *The Invisible Religion*. New York: Macmillan.

Maines, David R., and Monica J. Hardesty. 1982. "Anticipations of Work, Education, and Family Participation as Sex Differentiated Temporal Orders." Manuscript.

Matza, David. 1969. *Becoming Deviant*. Englewood Cliffs, N.J.: Prentice-Hall.

Miller, Donald E. 1975. "Religion, Social Change, and the Expansive Life Style." *International Yearbook for the Sociology of Knowledge and Religion* 9:149–59.

Nelsen, Hart M., Raytha L. Yokley, and Thomas W. Madron. 1973. "Ministerial Roles and Social Actionist Stance: Protestant Clergy and Protest in the Sixties." *American Sociological Review* 38:375–86.

Olesen, Virginia, and Elvi W. Whittaker. 1968. *The Silent Dialogue*. San Francisco, Ca.: Jossey-Bass.

————. 1970. "Critical Notes on Sociological Studies of Professional Socialization." In *Professions and Professionalization*, edited by J. A. Jackson, 179–221. London: Cambridge University Press.

Plant, Raymond. 1974. *Community and Ideology: An Essay in Applied Social Psychology*. London: Routledge and Kegan Paul.

Quinley, Harold E. 1974. *The Prophetic Clergy: Social Activism among Protestant Ministers*. New York: Wiley.

Rosow, Irving. 1965. "Forms and Functions of Adult Socialization." *Social Forces* 44:35–45.

Roth, Julius. 1974. "Professionalism: The Sociologist's Decoy." *Sociology of Work and Occupations* 1:6–23.

Sanders, Clinton R., and Eleanor Lyon. 1976. "The Humanistic Professional: The Reorientation of Artistic Production." In *Professions for the People: The Politics of Skill*, edited by J. E. Gerstl and G. Jacbos, 43–59. Cambridge, Mass.: Schenkman.

Sanford, Mark. 1976. *Making It in Graduate School*. Berkeley, Ca.: Montaigne.

Scheff, Thomas J. 1970. "Toward a Sociological Model of Consensus." In *Social Psychology through Symbolic Interaction*, edited by G. P. Stone and H. A. Farberman, 348–65. Waltham, Mass.: Ginn-Blaisdell.

Scheler, Max. 1961. *Ressentiment*. Edited by L. Coser, translated by H. Holdheim. New York: Free Press.

Schuller, D. S., M. L. Brekke, and M. P. Strommen. 1975. *Readiness for Ministry*. Vol. 1. Vandalia, Ohio: Association of Theological Schools in the United States and Canada.

Schur, Edwin. 1976. *The Awareness Trap*. New York: McGraw-Hill.

Schutz, Alfred. 1970. *On Phenomenology and Social Relations*. Chicago: University of Chicago Press.

Sennett, Richard. 1978. *The Fall of Public Man: On the Social Psychology of Capitalism*. New York: Vintage.

Shinn, Roger L. 1968. *New Directions in Theology Today*. Vol. 6. *Man: The New Humanism*. Philadelphia: Westminster Press.

Stone, Gregory P. 1970. "Appearance and the Self." In *Social Psychology through Symbolic Interaction*, edited by G. P. Stone and H. A. Farberman, 394–414. Waltham, Mass.: Ginn-Blaisdell.

Strauss, Anselm L. 1969. *Mirrors and Masks: The Search for Identity*. Sociology Press.

Swidler, Ann. 1979. *Organization without Authority: Dilemmas of Social Control in Free Schools*. Cambridge, Mass.: Harvard University Press.

Sykes, Gresham M. 1958. *The Society of Captives: A Study of a Maximum Security Prison*. Princeton, N.J.: Princeton University Press.

Toren, Nina. 1975. "Deprofessionalization and Its Sources." *Sociology of Work and Occupations* 2:323–37.

Turner, Ralph H. 1957. "The Normative Coherence of Folk Concepts." *Research Studies of the State College of Washington* 25:127–36.

———. 1976. "The Real Self: From Institution to Impulse." *American Journal of Sociology* 81:989–1016.

———. 1978. "The Role and the Person." *American Journal of Sociology* 84:1–23.

Varenne, Hervé. 1977. *Americans Together: Structured Diversity in a Midwestern Town*. New York: Teacher's College Press.

Wheeler, Stanton. 1966. "The Structure of Formally Organized Socialization Settings." In *Socialization after Childhood: Two Essays*, edited by Orville G. Brim, Jr., and Stanton Wheeler, 51–116. New York: Wiley.

Wilson, Bryan. 1976. *Contemporary Transformations of Religion*. London: Oxford University Press.

Winterowd, W. Ross. 1968. *Rhetoric: A Synthesis*. New York: Holt.

Wuthnow, Robert J. 1971. "New Forms of Religion in the Seminary." *Review of Religious Research* 12: 80–87.

INDEX

131